FLAUBERT IN EGYPT

A Sensibility on Tour

Flaubert in Egypt

A SENSIBILITY
ON TOUR

*A Narrative drawn from
Gustave Flaubert's
Travel Notes & Letters
translated from the French
& edited by
Francis Steegmuller*

ACADEMY
CHICAGO
LIMITED

© This selection and translation, Francis Steegmuller 1972

Academy Chicago Limited Edition 1979

Published by Academy Chicago Limited
360 North Michigan Avenue, Chicago, Il. 60601
All rights reserved
Printed and bound in the United States of America

Jacket: detail from *Women of Algiers,* by Eugène
Delacroix (Bulloz, Paris)

Flaubert, Gustave, 1821-1880.
   Flaubert in Egypt

   Bibliography: p.
   1. Egypt--Description and travel I. Steegmuller,
Francis, 1906 -   ed. II. Title.
DT54.F57 1979   916.2'04'3   79-17879
ISBN 0-89733-019-6
ISBN 0-89733-018-0 pbk.

CONTENTS

ILLUSTRATIONS

Flaubert as an adolescent. Drawing by Delaunay (*from* Flaubert par lui-même *by Victor Brombert. Aux Editions du Seuil, Paris*), pp. 8–9.

Maxime Du Camp. Drawing by E. Giraud (*from* Flaubert par lui-même *by Victor Brombert. Aux Editions du Seuil, Paris*), pp. 8–9.

Editor's Foreword

THE suggestion that such a book as this might be made was first broached to me one day by Graham Greene. He had been interested in those parts of Flaubert's Near-Eastern travel writings that had been included in an earlier book of mine, and asked whether there were more of the same. The present compilation was subsequently undertaken, and I hope that its Onlie Begetter and a few others may enjoy it. Primarily it is the record, to be read for pleasure, of a journey made by a young man of sensibility at the close of the Romantic Age—a journey in colorful country, made the more interesting by the reaction of the young man's temperament to his experiences.

As incidentals, the narrative may suggest partial answers to two questions that have long interested lovers of Flaubert.

It is well known that portions of these notes he made in Egypt bear a close relation to passages in the Carthaginian novel, *Salammbô*, the Palestinian tale, *Hérodias*, and the final version of his *Temptation of Saint Anthony*, all of which Flaubert wrote much later. But what indications are there, in the records of the Egyptian journey, that within little more than a year after its close this sensitive, sensual, Romantic young traveler would be writing *Madame Bovary*, the

Realist masterpiece that was to change the course of the novel throughout the western world ?

And—a lesser question—to what extent do Flaubert's recordings confirm the several writings about him and about the journey that came at various times from the pen of his much more worldly friend and companion, Maxime Du Camp ? Du Camp was also a young man of a certain sensibility, though his—I trust the reader will agree with me—is of a kind that throws Flaubert's into the most interesting relief: the sensibility of the novelist against that of the journalist. Some extracts from Du Camp's writings have been included here along with Flaubert's, in the hope that the juxtaposition may be illuminating.

Du Camp published several travel books. Not so Flaubert. 'I had urged him,' Du Camp wrote later, 'to write up the Greek portion of our journey; it could make a short, interesting book, excellent for a début in letters. He rejected my advice, saying that travel, like the humanities, should serve only to "enliven one's style," and that incidents gleaned abroad might be used in a novel, but not in a straight account. Travel writings were to him the same as news items, he said, a low form of literature, and he had higher aspirations.' What Flaubert did was to save his travel notes, and even to re-write some of them; and other people saved his letters. Selections from these comprise the bulk of the present volume.

F. S.

1. Flaubert as an adolescent. (Apart from the photograph facing p. 40, there are no known pictures of Flaubert in his twenties.)

2. Maxime Du Camp, 'Father of Thinness'
(see p. 102).

I

The Background of the Journey

THE Gustave Flaubert who left France in the autumn of 1849 for a long tour of the 'Orient' (a term then often used to denote what we now call the Near and Middle East, and even North Africa) was a young man approaching twenty-eight, unknown outside his own circle, but who impressed friends and strangers alike by his size, his beauty, and his air of athletic vigor. (The only testimony to this is verbal: there are no clear pictures of Flaubert at this time of his life.) He was almost six feet tall, muscular, a blond 'Viking,' born in Rouen in Normandy, with large dark eyes and a mouth so fine that, as he was to write from Egypt, women there invariably reproached him for hiding its charms under a moustache.

He was a sensualist, but of a particular kind. When he was fifteen, he had fallen romantically in love with a married woman eleven years older than himself, and he sometimes said that he continued to be romantically in love with her always. He was a great frequenter of prostitutes, and about prostitution he entertained a particular *mystique*. 'It may be a perverted taste,' he was to write, 'but I love prostitution, and for itself, too, quite apart from its carnal aspects. My heart begins to pound every time I see one of those women in low-cut dresses walking under the lamplight in the rain, just as monks in their corded robes have always excited some deep, ascetic corner of my soul. The idea of prostitution is a meeting place of so many elements—lust, bitterness, complete absence of human contact, muscular frenzy, the clink of gold—that to peer into it deeply makes one reel. One learns so many things in a brothel, and feels such sadness, and dreams so longingly of love! . . .'

The human body held no secrets for him—he was the son of a surgeon, knew many doctors and even the dissecting room of his father's hospital. Before setting out for Egypt he had broken off an affair of several years with another married woman, this one a beautiful blue-stocking named Louise Colet, also eleven years older than he, to whom he had written quantities of eloquent letters, erotic and literary, which her daughter later sold and which have been printed. He wrote to his mistress far more often than he saw her, however, and large parts of the letters are explanations of why their meetings must be postponed. His most intense affection was for others: for his mother, and for a few men friends of his own age, one of whom, the most beloved, Alfred Le Poittevin, a gifted young Romantic like himself, had recently half broken Flaubert's heart by dying—a victim of tuberculosis and of the *mal du siècle*, ennui. (Le Poittevin's had been the latest in a series of deaths—in 1849 Flaubert was emerging from a period of mourning: during the previous few years he had lost two more of those closest to him—his father, and his sister Caroline Hamard, who had left a baby girl, also named Caroline, now removed from her irresponsible father and being brought up by Madame Flaubert and Gustave himself in their old white country house on the river Seine at Croisset outside Rouen.)

In short, Flaubert's bluff, athletic exterior and the more conventional of his amorous exploits were misleading; he was one of the world's great sensitives, and while reluctantly, at his father's insistence, attending law school in Paris, he had suffered a series of epileptic attacks that had forced him—allowed him, rather—to abandon legal studies and live quietly at home and do what he most wanted to do—write.

For Gustave Flaubert had always written: he began to compose, he once said, as soon as he could form letters. Approaching twenty-eight, he had in his desk the manuscripts of countless youthful short stories, two novels, an account of a walking tour in Brittany, and a long dramatic fantasy called *The Temptation of Saint Anthony*—all—except two of the stories—unpublished, and not even offered for publication.

Like many of his contemporaries who were children or adolescents in the Romantic Age, Flaubert had been infected with a longing for the exotic, especially by his reading of Byron, Victor Hugo's *Les Orientales*, and the *Arabian Nights*. His early writings are full of yearning for the East: 'Oh, how willingly I would give up all the women in the world to possess the mummy of Cleopatra!' is a sample of his youthful 'oriental' effusions; and his *Temptation of Saint Anthony* was the maturer culmination of them, completed just before he left for Egypt—an evocation of the saint in his cave in the Egyptian Thebaid, assailed by hordes of monsters, gods, heretics and other sinners. Flaubert the student in gray northern Rouen had always had a strong taste for the sun and for classical antiquity; he was a fair Latinist and knew some Greek; it seems to have been his reading of

Herodotus that first showed him the way to oriental antiquity; for *Saint Anthony* he had been reading about eastern religions; gradually his interest in the 'Orient' had broadened into something more than a mere taste for the picturesque. It was no mere idle sightseer who was about to visit the 'East.' As Jean Bruneau has put it: 'His love of the sun, which is the key to his pantheism; his taste for antiquity, which led to his discovery of the ancient Orient; his curiosity concerning religions—all this resulted in a deepening of his idea of the Orient and gave it an even more prominent place in his meditations and writings. . . . Flaubert's Orient is no mere dreamlike décor, no mere source of local color . . . For Flaubert the Orient gradually became a kind of homeland.'

But, even though when he was there he was to experience many a sense of '*déjà vu*,' it remained, until 1849, a 'homeland' that he had never seen.

One of his closest remaining friends, Maxime Du Camp, whom he met while he was studying law and suffering his first epileptic seizures, was more fortunate. Wealthy and an orphan, he could do much as he liked; in his early twenties he traveled alone to Asia Minor, Italy and Algeria; and in 1848, at the age of twenty-six, he published his memoirs of that journey, *Souvenirs et Paysages d'Orient*, which he dedicated to '*G. F., S ad S*'—'*Gustave Flaubert: Solus ad Solum*.' Flaubert wrote him that his hands 'trembled with joy' as he cut its pages. It was Du Camp, slight, dark, vivacious, ambitious, devoted and energetic, who encouraged Flaubert—whose tendency to be sedentary was now beginning to weaken his Eastern longings—to accompany him on a second, longer journey that he wanted to make; and it was the efficient Du Camp who persuaded Madame Flaubert, the most anxious of mothers, to agree to her son's departure and give him the necessary money. This Du Camp finally accomplished, after long efforts, by getting a friend of the Flauberts, Dr Jules Cloquet, a celebrated anatomist with whom Gustave at eighteen had traveled in the Pyrenees and in Corsica, to assure Madame Flaubert that a visit to warm countries would benefit Gustave's health.

Also on the scene was the second of Flaubert's remaining close young friends, whose circumstances contrasted sharply with those of Flaubert himself and of Du Camp. This was Louis Bouilhet, a quiet unpublished poet of slender means who had abandoned medical studies and was earning his living as a tutor in Rouen. Like Flaubert, Bouilhet was a lover of antiquity, and in 1849 he was writing, among other things, a long poem, *Melaenis*, set in ancient Rome. He and Flaubert saw each other constantly and exchanged literary counsel. It was Du Camp who first told, in his *Souvenirs Littéraires* (published in the 1880s, after Flaubert's death), of the all-night session, shortly before the Egyptian journey, during which Flaubert read aloud to him and Bouilhet his just-completed *Temptation of Saint Anthony* and the two friends roundly 'condemned' the extravaganza, urging Flaubert not to try to publish it. Du Camp's account continues as follows:

'During the day that followed that sleepless night we were sitting silently in the garden, saddened by the thought of Flaubert's disappointment and the truths that we had not spared him. Suddenly Bouilhet said: "Why shouldn't you write the story of Delaunay?" Flaubert sat up and exclaimed happily: "What a good idea!"

'Delaunay was a poor devil of a medical officer

who had studied under Flaubert's father and whom
we had known. He married his first wife, an older
woman, under the false impression that she was rich,
and after her death a penniless young woman who
had acquired a slight polish in a boarding school at
Rouen. She was petite and plain, with dull blond
hair framing a freckled face; and she was pretentious,
looking down on her husband, whom she considered a
fool. White-skinned and plump, her fine bones well
padded, she moved and walked with an almost snake-
like sinuousness. This impression was strengthened
by her voice, which had something insinuating about
it despite her unpleasant Low Norman accent; and in
her eyes—of indefinable color, appearing green, gray
or blue, according to the light—there was a perpetual
pleading look. Delaunay worshipped his wife, who
cared nothing about him; she took lovers right and
left and found no satisfaction anywhere. She was the
victim of an acute neurosis, the kind that wrecks the
anemic. Afflicted with nymphomania, an obsessive
spender, she acted irresponsibly, and none of this
was cured by the only medicine she was given—good
advice. Debt-ridden, pursued by her creditors, beaten
by her lovers—for whose benefit she robbed her
husband—she poisoned herself in a fit of despair. She
left a small daughter, whom Delaunay determined to
bring up as best he could; but the poor man, ruined,
pointed at, using up his all in a vain effort to pay his
wife's debts, in his turn lost all taste for life. He prepared some cyanide of potassium and rejoined the
woman whose loss had left him disconsolate.

'It was that intimate drama, enacted by four or five
characters in an obscure country town, that Bouilhet
suggested to Flaubert: he eagerly agreed, and it
became *Madame Bovary*. It is certain that Flaubert

would never have thought of writing that novel if he had been satisfied with *The Temptation of Saint Anthony*.'

Because it has become known that 'Delaunay' (his real name was Eugène Delamare: Du Camp had disguised it, apparently to protect either himself or the daughter) did not die until after Flaubert had left for Egypt, and that only after his return did Bouilhet suggest that he make use of the material, Du Camp's narrative of the 'condemnation' scene cannot be accepted in detail; and after the publication of his *Souvenirs* Du Camp quickly earned the dislike of early Flaubertistes for other reasons as well—among them his being the first to speak in print of Flaubert's epilepsy. (This was considered disloyal, a 'betrayal,' by Flaubert's surviving friends and admirers.) Nevertheless, Du Camp's various writings (shortly after his and Flaubert's return from Egypt he published a second travel book, *Le Nil, Egypte et Nubie*) are among the most important sources of information concerning Flaubert; and Jean Bruneau, the best-qualified appraiser of the matter, is of the opinion that 'Du Camp deforms reality, but cannot be accused of deliberate lying.'

Such, in brief, is the background of Flaubert's Egyptian journey; and four of the persons figuring in that background are the central characters of the journey itself: the travelers Flaubert and Du Camp, and the stay-at-homes Madame Flaubert and Bouilhet, who received Flaubert's letters. (There is one letter to Dr Cloquet, and Flaubert wrote a few letters to others that have not been included.) In addition, the cast includes two characters whom Flaubert calls the 'mutes'—a servant, a Corsican ex-dragoon named

Sassetti, engaged in Paris by Du Camp, and their Genoa-born dragoman, hired in Cairo, Giuseppe Brichetti, whose name was gallicised by the travelers, to simple 'Joseph.' And in all but the first scenes there is the crew of the '*cange*,' the Nile boat, all of whom—there were about a dozen—are described by Du Camp.* Assorted officials, priests, mountebanks, dancers and prostitutes appear and disappear as the travelers move about in Cairo and up and down the Nile; and always in the background, 'far away, on a river gentler and less ancient than this,' beside a 'long terrace, Louis XIV, bordered with lindens,' is young Flaubert's study at Croisset, waiting for him to return and write—what?

Du Camp is certainly mistaken if his words about *Madame Bovary* were meant to imply that until Bouilhet spoke of the Delamares Flaubert had never thought of writing a novel of French provincial life. His Breton walking tour two years before (which he had made with Du Camp) had taken him through Blois, on the Loire; and in his note about that quiet city he had described a thought that had come to him there:

'At Blois the streets are empty, grass grows between the cobbles; down both sides stretch long gray walls enclosing large gardens, with here and there a discreet little door that gives the impression of being opened only at night, to mysterious visitors. You feel that all the days must be the same here; that in this calm monotony—which nevertheless has its own sweetness, like the sound of church bells striking the hour—they must be full of exquisite melancholy and tender longings. One likes to imagine some deep, great, intimate story being lived here amid these

* See Appendix, 'The Crew of the Cange.'

peaceful dwellings, a passion like a sickness, lasting until death, the unavowed, life-long love that one finds in a pious old maid or a virtuous wife; one can't help thinking that this would be just the place for some pale beauty with long nails and delicate hands, a high-born, cold-mannered lady married to a boor, a miser, a jealous husband, and who is dying of consumption.'

It is the young writer who 'likes to imagine' that kind of a story, as well as the Romantic who had just completed *The Temptation of Saint Anthony*, whom we are about to accompany to his dreamed-of 'Orient.'

II

Croisset to Cairo

*During all his Near-Eastern journey Flaubert jotted
down his impressions in a series of pocket-size notebooks,
which still exist. (See Bibliographical Note, p. 229.)
After his return he copied and expanded his entries, and
in the text of the present volume it is often possible to
detect the later additions, which give the reader a sensa-
tion of moving back and forth in time.*

*It was with his mother and three-year-old niece that
Flaubert set out from Croisset on the first stage of the
journey to Egypt. Madame Flaubert was to spend some
time in Nogent with cousins rather than remain in the
'empty' house at Croisset.*

FROM FLAUBERT'S TRAVEL NOTES

I left Croisset on Monday, 22 October 1849. Of those
of the household who bade me goodbye only Bossière,
the gardener, seemed to me to be really moved. For me
the moment of emotion had come two days before, on
Saturday, when I put away my pens and papers. The
weather was neither good nor bad. At the [Rouen]
station, my sister-in-law and her daughter; also
Bouilhet . . . The next day we had dinner [in Paris]
with Monsieur Cloquet. My mother was doleful
throughout the meal . . . Wednesday at four o'clock
we left for Nogent. My uncle Parain kept us waiting a

long time and I was afraid we might miss the train, which would have seemed a bad omen.

... The next day, Thursday—atrocious day, the worst I have ever spent. I was not supposed to leave [for Paris, en route to Marseilles] until the day after the next, but I decided to go at once; it was unbearable. Endless strolls with my mother in the little garden. I set my departure for five; the clock seemed to stand still. I put my hat in the living-room and sent my trunk on ahead to the station; it would take me only a minute to get there. As for local callers, I remember Mme Dainez, the postmistress. Also M. Morin, in charge of the mail coach, who as he left shook hands with me over the gate, saying: 'You're going to see a great country, a great religion, a great people,' etc., and much more such palaver.

Finally I got away. My mother was sitting in an armchair beside the fire, and in the midst of caressing her and talking with her I suddenly kissed her on the forehead, rushed from the room, seized my hat, and ran out of the house. How she screamed when I closed the door of the living-room behind me! It reminded me of her scream just after the death of my father, when she took his hand.

My eyes were dry; I felt a kind of constriction around my heart, but little emotion except nervousness and even a kind of anger; my face must have looked set. I lit a cigar, and Bonenfant [my cousin] ran out and joined me. He spoke to me of the necessity, the advisability, of making a will, and of leaving a power-of-attorney because some disaster might overtake my mother in my absence, etc. I have never experienced such a feeling of hatred towards anyone as towards him at that moment. God has probably forgiven him for the wrong he did me, but the memory of it will always remain. He nearly drove me mad, and yet I stopped him politely!

At the station entrance, a priest and four nuns: bad omen! All afternoon a dog in the neighborhood had been howling dismally. I envy strong-minded men who don't notice such things at those moments.

My uncle Parain said nothing to me at all—a proof of his big heart. I shall always be more grateful to him for his silence than for any great service he could do me.

In the waiting-room there was a gentleman (a business acquaintance of Bonenfant's) who was deploring the fate of dogs in trains. 'They are with unknown dogs who give them fleas; the small dogs are trampled on by the big ones; one would rather pay a little more,' etc. Suddenly Eugénie appeared, in tears: 'Monsieur Parain! Madame wants you, she is having hysterics!' And they went off.

From Nogent to Paris. What a ride! I closed the windows (I was alone in the compartment), held my handkerchief to my mouth, and wept. After a time the sound of my own voice (which reminded me of Dorval* two or three times) brought me to myself, then the sobs began again. At one point my head was spinning so that I was afraid. 'Calm down! Calm down!' I opened the window; the moon, surrounded by a halo of mist, was shining in puddles; it was cold. I thought of my mother, her face all contracted from weeping, the droop at the corners of her mouth . . .

At Montereau I went into the station restaurant and drank three or four glasses of rum, not to try to forget things, but just to do something, anything.

* Flaubert had doubtless seen and heard the great actress Marie Dorval in Romantic plays by Hugo, de Vigny and Dumas *père*.

Then my misery took another form: I thought of returning. (At every station I was on the point of getting off; only the fear of being a coward prevented me.) I imagined the voice of Eugénie, crying: 'Madame! It's Monsieur Gustave!' I could give my mother this tremendous joy at once; it was up to me entirely. I lulled myself with this idea; I was exhausted, and it relaxed me.

Arrival in Paris: interminable wait for my baggage. I cross the city, via the Marais and the Place Royale. I had to make up my mind before arriving at Maxime's. He was out. Aimée lets me in, tries to stir up the fire. Maxime returns at midnight. I was exhausted and completely undecided. He left it up to me, and finally I decided not to return to Nogent. At one in the morning, after hours of sobbing and anguish such as no other separation ever caused me, I wrote a letter. I have it now: I have just re-read it and am holding it in my hand, quite without emotion; its paper gives no hint that it is different from any other piece of paper, and the letters are like any other letters in any other sentences. Between my self of that night and my self of tonight* there is the difference between the cadaver and the surgeon doing the autopsy.

The next two days I lived lavishly—huge dinners, quantities of wine, whores. The senses are not far removed from the emotions, and my poor tortured nerves needed a little relaxation.

* When he was copying and expanding his notes, two years later.

Paris, 26 October 1849 one a.m.
[Night of 25–26].

You are probably sleeping now, poor old darling. How you must have wept tonight—I did too, believe me! Tell me how you are—*keep nothing from me.* Think, poor darling, of how terrible my remorse would be if this trip were distressing to you. Max is very kind; have no fear. I found our passports ready. Everything has gone like clockwork, and that's a good sign. Goodbye—this is my first letter; there will soon be others. Tomorrow I'll send you a longer one. And you? Write me volumes: *pour out everything.* Goodbye—I love you with all my heart: it is full of you.

Flaubert wrote his mother four more letters even before leaving Paris: then one from Lyons, and two from Marseilles before sailing for Egypt, via Malta, on November 4th. In one of them he says: 'It is fully agreed between Max and me that if, once we have seen Egypt, we are worn out, or I miss you too much, or you ask me to come back, I'll come. So—don't torment yourself in advance.'

FROM THE 'SOUVENIRS LITTÉRAIRES'
OF MAXIME DU CAMP

(*It should be kept in mind that Du Camp's* Souvenirs Littéraires *were not written until after Flaubert's death in 1880, thirty years after the Egyptian journey.*)

I wanted us to enjoy every possible advantage while traveling, and had asked the government to give us a mission that would recommend us to French diplomatic and commercial agents in the Orient. Need I say that this mission was to be, and was, entirely unpaid? My request was granted. Flaubert—it is hard not to smile—was charged by the Ministry of Agriculture and Commerce with the task of collecting, in the various ports and caravan centers, any information that he thought might interest Chambers of Commerce. I was given something better—a mission from the Ministry of Public Instruction, where I knew François Génin, who was at that time head of the division of sciences and letters.

The following officially couched remarks concerning Du Camp and his mission were indited by the Institut de France (Académie des Inscriptions et Belles-lettres) at its meeting of September 7th 1849:

'*In requesting instructions intended to guide him in the journey he is to undertake, M. Maxime Du Camp told the Academy that he will be equipped with an apparatus (photographic) for the purpose of securing, along his way and with the aid of this marvelous means of reproduction, views of the monuments and copies of the inscriptions. Thanks to the aid of this modern traveling companion, efficient, rapid, and always scrupulously exact, the results of M. Du Camp's journey may well be quite special in character and extremely important. Quite apart from the use of photographic procedures, M. Du Camp will do well to equip himself with the best possible devices for the securing of facsimiles of the inscriptions in their actual size.*'*

The last sentence refers to the 'squeezes'—mouldings

* With the Du Camp papers in the Bibliothèque de l'Institut. (See Bibliographical Note, p. 229.) Flaubert's instructions from the Ministry of Commerce, a fantastically bureaucratic document, are in the Archives Nationales.

*or casts of inscriptions and reliefs obtained by the applica-
tion of wet paper—whose execution was to prove so
boring to Flaubert. Du Camp had even had a map of
Egypt drawn and printed, showing the principal intended stopping places. A copy of this was left with
Madame Flaubert, so that she might follow her son's
progress.*

. . . We were to leave Paris on the twenty-ninth of
October. Flaubert had taken his mother to her family
at Nogent-sur-Seine, and on the twenty-sixth he
came to stay with me. I had not been aware that he
intended to come, but when I returned home that
evening my servant told me he had arrived.

I did not see him at first when I entered my study,
but after a moment I saw that he was stretched out at
full length on a black bearskin in front of the bookcase.
I thought he was asleep, but then I heard him sigh. I
have never beheld such a state of prostration, and his
size and appearance of physical strength made it all
the more remarkable. When I questioned him he
replied with lamentations:

'Never again will I see my mother or my country!
This journey is too long, too distant; it is tempting
fate! What madness! Why are we going?' I was dis-
mayed. He told me that he had left his study at
Croisset exactly as though he were going to return
to it the next day—on the table a book open at the
page he had last read, his dressing-gown thrown over a
chair, his slippers near the sofa. 'It is unlucky to take
precautions,' he told me; and then, referring to the
[recent] death of my grandmother, said cruelly: 'You
are lucky; you leave no one behind.'

I let him spend the night in this state of discouragement, but the next morning before he was up I went

into his room. 'There is nothing that obliges you to leave with me,' I said. 'If you think the trip is more than you can do, you ought to give it up. I will go alone.' The struggle was brief. 'No!' he cried. 'I'd be so ridiculous that I'd never dare look at myself in the mirror again.'

The arrival of Bouilhet and my friend Louis de Cormenin, who came to keep us company during the last days, was a diversion for him. He threw off his languor and was himself again.

From the moment Flaubert decided to come with me, I had had to change not the itinerary but the conditions of the trip. The state of his health was far less flourishing than his splendid appearance seemed to indicate, and it could cause us serious trouble; he always had to be watched over, and that was something it would be hard for me to manage alone. I therefore decided to take with me my man-servant, a Corsican by birth, a former dragoon named Sassetti. I was sure of his devotion, and knew I could count on him in difficult circumstances; he would be able to stand in for me with Flaubert whenever emergencies of work or travel might take me briefly away. This would involve extra expense, but it would provide extra security, and I made the decision unhesitatingly.

On the twenty-eighth we had a farewell dinner. Théophile Gautier, Louis de Cormenin, Bouilhet, Flaubert and I dined in one of the private rooms of the restaurant Les Trois Frères Provençaux, in the Palais Royal, and spent the evening talking of art, literature, and the ancient world. Flaubert, very keyed up, spoke of discovering the sources of the Nile. Gautier urged me to become a Moslem, that I might wear silken robes and kiss the black stone at Mecca. Louis de Cormenin was sad because of my departure, and Bouilhet silently gnawed the end of his cigar after enjoining us to think of him if we should find ourselves in the presence of some relic of Cleopatra. When we separated, we said affectionate farewells.

The express did not exist in those days, and it was a long journey from Paris to Marseilles. On the twenty-ninth we took the stage-coach, then the steamer from Chalon to Lyons, then the Rhône boat as far as Valence, where we were stopped by fog, then a post-chaise to Avignon, and finally the railroad, which took us to Marseilles on November first. It was at this time that I began the habit of writing down every night what I had done during the day—a habit to which I have always been faithful and which guarantees the accuracy of these memoirs. On the fourth, in overcast, dirty weather we boarded the *Nil*, a steam packet of 250 horse-power which rolled like a drunken man and made but little headway.

I cannot say that Flaubert had no recurrence of his melancholy. He stood for a long time leaning against the rail, gazing at the coast of Provence as it gradually disappeared into the fog. After eleven days of rolling and pitching, of wind and heavy seas, we sighted the shore of Egypt, and on Saturday the fifteenth of November 1849 we disembarked at Alexandria.

FLAUBERT TO HIS MOTHER

Malta. On board the Nil.
Night of Wednesday–Thursday,
7–8 November [*1849*].
. . . Do you know something, poor darling, something wonderful? I haven't been seasick (except for the first half hour after leaving Marseilles, when I vomited a glass of rum I had drunk to *prevent* my

being sick) . . . I've spent my time walking on deck, dining with the ship's officers, standing on the gangway between the two paddle-wheels with the captain, striking attitudes *à la* Jean Bart,* with my cap on one side and cigar in my mouth . . . When it grows dark I watch the sea and daydream, draped in my pelisse like Childe Harold. In short I'm on top of the world. I don't know why, but I'm adored on board.

. . . One of the most comical-looking faces is Maxime's. He didn't expect to be sick, poor fellow, and recommended me to the attention of the ship's doctor, whereas I haven't had a moment's discomfort and he scarcely stops suffering for a second. As to his servant, Sassetti, he puts on a bold front, but he is hardly any steadier on his feet than his master . . .

Flaubert and Du Camp were to find various official doors open to them in Egypt, and that would probably have been the case even had they not been 'chargés de mission': it was their French nationality that counted. France had maintained a controlling political interest in Egypt despite the fall of Napoleon (whom the Egyptians had called 'Sultan Kebir'—'Great Sultan'); it was French influence that in 1841 persuaded the Turkish Sultan, Abdu'l-Mejid, nominally Egypt's ruler, to confer hereditary sovereignty of Egypt on the family of his viceroy, Mohammed Ali, who died only a few months before Flaubert's arrival. Mohammed Ali had taken many Frenchmen into his service and conferred on some of them the title of Bey, or occasionally Pasha. Soliman Pasha, for example, mentioned in the following letter, was a former French army colonel named Sève, who with Mohammed Ali's son Ibrahim Pasha had helped defeat the forces of the Sultan (against whom Mohammed Ali

* A seventeenth-century naval hero.

was at that time in revolt) at the battle of Nezib, in 1839.
Galis Bey and Princeteau Bey, also mentioned, were
likewise French. (Lauvergne was a French doctor in
Toulon, who had known Sève there.) The welcome
extended to Flaubert by these officials would reassure his
mother—that was his purpose in writing her about them
—but Flaubert himself was thinking of some of them
when he wrote later to Louis Bouilhet: 'The French
canaille *abroad is impressive—and, let me add, there is a*
lot of it.' Other Frenchborn Egyptian officials will be
found mentioned from time to time in the notes and
letters: Lambert Bey (Charles Lambert), engineer and
Saint-Simonian; Mougel Bey, another engineer; Lub-
bert Bey, court chamberlain; Clot Bey (Antoine Clot),
doctor; Bekir Bey, a Corsican, chief of the Egyptian
'police des étrangers.' Not all were canaille *by any*
means—Lambert, a high-minded man, was to exercise a
lasting influence on Du Camp by turning him toward
social journalism and ideas of 'progress,' and Clot was a
splendid medical officer—but there were adventurers
among them.

The Viceroy of Egypt in late 1849 was Abbas Pasha,
grandson of Mohammed Ali, Ibrahim Pasha having died
before his father.

FLAUBERT TO HIS MOTHER

Alexandria, 17 November 1849
. . . When we were two hours out from the coast of
Egypt I went into the bow with the chief quarter-
master and saw the seraglio of Abbas Pasha like a
black dome on the blue of the Mediterranean. The
sun was beating down on it. I had my first sight of the
Orient through, or rather in, a glowing light that was
like melted silver on the sea. Soon the shore became

distinguishable, and the first thing we saw on land was a pair of camels led by their driver; then, on the dock, some Arabs peacefully fishing. Landing took place amid the most deafening uproar imaginable: negroes, negresses, camels, turbans, cudgelings to right and left, and ear-splitting guttural cries. I gulped down a whole bellyful of colors, like a donkey filling himself with hay. Cudgelings play a great role here; everyone who wears clean clothes beats everyone who wears dirty ones, or rather none at all, and when I say clothes I mean a pair of short breeches. You see many gentlemen sauntering along the streets with nothing but a shirt and a long pipe. Except in the very lowest classes, all the women are veiled, and in their noses they wear ornaments that hang down and sway from side to side like the facedrops of a horse. On the other hand, if you don't see their faces, you see their entire bosoms. As you change countries, you find that modesty changes its location, like a bored traveler who keeps shifting from the outside to the inside of the stage-coach. One curious thing here is the respect, or rather the terror, that everyone displays in the presence of 'Franks,' as they call Europeans. We have had bands of ten or twelve Arabs, advancing across the whole width of a street, break apart to let us pass. In fact, Alexandria is almost a European city, there are so many Europeans here. At table in our hotel alone there are thirty, and the place is full of Englishmen, Italians, etc. Yesterday we saw a magnificent procession celebrating the circumcision of the son of a rich merchant. This morning we saw Cleopatra's Needles (two great obelisks on the shorefront), Pompey's column, the catacombs, and Cleopatra's baths. Tomorrow we leave for Rosetta, whence we shall return in three or four days. We go slowly and don't get overtired, living sensibly and clad in flannel from head to foot, even though the temperature indoors is sometimes thirty degrees.* The heat is not at all unbearable, thanks to the sea breeze.

Soliman Pasha, the most powerful man in Egypt, the terror of Constantinople—he won the battle of Nezib—happens just now to be in Alexandria instead of Cairo. We paid him a visit yesterday, and presented Lauvergne's letter. He received us very graciously. He is to give us orders for all the provincial governors of Egypt and offered us his carriage for the journey to Cairo. It was he who arranged about our horses for tomorrow. He is charming, cordial, etc. He apparently likes the way we look. In addition, we have M. Galis, chief of the army engineers, Princeteau Bey, etc., just to give you an idea of how we are to travel. We have been given soldiers to hold back the crowd when we want to photograph: I trust you are impressed. As you see, poor old darling, conditions couldn't be better. As for ophthalmia, of the people one sees only the very lowest orders (as the expression goes) suffer from it. M. Willemin, a young doctor who has been in Egypt five years, told us this morning that he has not seen a single case among the well-to-do or Europeans. That should reassure you. Don't worry, I'll come back in good shape. I have put on so much weight since I left that two pairs of my trousers are with M. Chavannes, a French tailor, being let out to accommodate my paunch.

So—goodbye, old lady. I was interrupted during the writing of this letter by the arrival of M. Pastré, the banker who is to send us our money as we need it and will ship home any packages, in case we buy a

* Réaumur. 86° Fahrenheit.

mummy or two. Now we are going to our friend Soliman Pasha to pick up a letter from him about tomorrow's expedition: it is addressed to the Governor of Rosetta, seeing to it that he puts us up in his house—i.e., in the fort, apparently the only place to stay. We had intended to push on as far as Damietta. But as we have been told that that would be too tiring on horseback because of the sand, we have given up the idea. We'll go to Cairo by boat. As you see, we're not stubborn; it's our principle to follow the advice of experts and to behave like a pair of little saints. Goodbye, a thousand kisses, kiss the baby for me, send me long letters . . .

THE SAME TO THE SAME

Alexandria, Thursday, 22 [*November 1849*]
My darling—I am writing you in white tie and tails, pumps, etc., like a man who has been paying a call on a prime minister: in fact we have just left Hartim Bey, Minister of Foreign Affairs, to whom we were introduced by the [French] consul and who received us splendidly. He is going to give us a *firman* with his seal on it for our entire journey. It is unbelievable how well we are treated here—it's as though we were princes, and I'm not joking. Sassetti keeps saying: 'Whatever happens, I'll be able to say that once in my life I had ten slaves to serve me and one to chase away the flies,' and that is quite true.

. . . Friday morning. [*23 November.*]
We set out at daybreak last Sunday, saddled and booted, harnessed and armed, with four men running behind us, our dragoman on his mule carrying our coats and supplies, and our three horses, which were

ridden with simple halters. They looked like nags but were on the contrary excellent beasts; with two pricks of the spur they were off at a gallop, and a whistle brought them up short. To make them go right or left you had only to touch their neck. The desert begins at the very gates of Alexandria: first sandy hillocks covered here and there with palms, and then dunes that stretch on endlessly. From time to time you see on the horizon what looks like great stretches of water with trees reflected in them, and at their farthest limit, where they seem to touch the sky, a gray vapor that appears to be moving in a rush, like a train: that is the mirage, known to all, Arabs and Europeans—people familiar with the desert as well as those seeing it for the first time. Now and then you come upon the carcass of some animal on the sand—a dead camel three-quarters eaten by jackals, its guts exposed and blackened by the sun; a mummified buffalo, a horse's head, etc. Arabs trot by on their donkeys, their wives bundled in immense black or white veils: you exchange greetings—' Taïeb '—and continue on your way. About eleven o'clock we lunched near Abukir, in a fort manned by soldiers who gave us excellent coffee and refused *baksheesh* (a wonder!). The beach at Abukir is in places still littered with the wreckage of ships.* We saw a number of sharks that had been washed up, and our horses trod on shells at the edge of the sea. We shot cormorants and water-magpies, and our Arabs ran like hares to pick up those we wounded: I brought down a few birds myself—yes, *me*!—something new, what? The weather was magnificent, sea and sky bluest blue, an immensity of space.

* From the naval battle of August 1st 1798, when Nelson destroyed the French fleet?

At a place called Edku (you will find it on your map) we took a ferry and there our runners bought some dates from a camel-driver whose two beasts were laden with them. A mile or two farther on, we were riding tranquilly along side by side, a hundred feet in front of our runners, when suddenly we heard loud cries from behind. We turned, and saw our men in a tumult, jostling and pushing one another and making signs for us to turn back. Sassetti dashed off at a gallop, his velvet jacket streaming out behind him; and digging our spurs into our horses we followed after to the scene of the conflict. It was occasioned, we discovered, by the owner of the dates, who had been following his camels at a distance and who, coming upon our men and seeing that they were eating dates, had thought they had stolen them and had fallen on them with his cudgel.

But when he saw us three ruffians descending upon him with rifles slung over our saddles, roles were reversed, and from the beater he became the beaten. Courage returned to our men, and they fell upon him with their sticks in such a way that his backside was soon resounding with blow after blow. To escape, he ran into the sea, lifting up his robe to keep it dry, but his assailants followed. The higher he lifted his robe, the greater the area he exposed to their cudgels, which rattled on him like drumsticks. You can't imagine anything funnier than that man's black behind amidst the white foam churned up by the combat. The rest of us stood on the shore, laughing like fools; my sides still ache when I think of it . . . Two days later, coming back from Rosetta, we met the same camels as they were returning from Alexandria. Perceiving us from afar, the owner hastily left his beasts and made a long detour in the desert to avoid us—a precaution which diverted us considerably. You would scarcely believe the important role played by the cudgel in this part of the world; buffets are distributed with a sublime prodigality, always accompanied by loud cries; it's the most genuine kind of local color you can think of.

At six in the evening, after a sunset that made the sky look like melted vermilion and the sand of the desert like ink, we arrived at Rosetta and found all the gates closed. At the name of Soliman Pasha they opened, creaking faintly like the doors of a barn. The streets were dark, and so narrow that there was just room for a single horseman. We rode through the bazaars, where each shop was lit by a glass of oil hanging from a cord, and arrived at the barracks. The Pasha received us on his sofa, surrounded by negroes who brought us pipes and coffee. After many courtesies and compliments, we were given supper and shown to our beds, which were equipped with excellent mosquito-netting . . . The next morning while we were washing the Pasha came into our room, followed by the regimental doctor, an Italian who spoke French perfectly and did us the honors of the city. Thanks to him we spent a very agreeable day. When he learned my name and that I was the son of a doctor, he said he had heard of Father and had often seen his name cited. It was no small satisfaction to me, dear Mother, to think that Father's memory was still useful to me, serving as a kind of protection at this distance. That reminds me that in the depths of Brittany, too, at Guérande, the local doctor told me he had quoted Father in his thesis. Yes, poor darling, I think constantly of those who are gone; as my body continues on its journey, my thoughts keep turning back and bury themselves in days past.

. . . All morning was taken up with things to do in Rosetta. By the way, when you write to Rouen will you please make inquiries about M. Julienne, who invented those fuel-saving devices for steam pumps? What is his address? Would he like to enter into correspondence with M. Foucault, manager of rice production at Rosetta, to whom I spoke of this invention and who would like to hear more? . . . I promised to do this, and would like to keep my word . . .

That was one of Flaubert's very rare references to anything that might be thought of as relating to his 'mission.' Nevertheless, in this same letter he urges his mother, when addressing her envelopes to him, to write 'my name, title, and "Cairo, Egypt"'—the 'title' being: 'Chargé d'une mission en Orient.'

FROM FLAUBERT'S TRAVEL NOTES

Sunday morning, 25 [November 1849]
From Alexandria to Cairo. Leave on a boat towed by a small steamer carrying only its engine. Flat, dead banks of the Mahmudiyeh; on the shore a few naked Arabs running, from time to time, a traveler trots by on horseback, swathed in white in his Turkish saddle. Passengers: . . . an English family, hideous; the mother looks like a sick old parrot (because of the green eyeshade attached to her bonnet) . . . At 'Atfeh you enter the Nile and take a larger boat.

First night on the Nile. State of contentment and of lyricism: I gesticulate, recite lines from Bouilhet, cannot bring myself to go to bed; I think of Cleopatra. The water is yellow and very smooth; a few stars. Well wrapped in my pelisse, I fall asleep on my camp-bed, on deck. Such rapture! I awoke before Maxime; in waking, he stretched out his left hand instinctively, to see if I was there.

On one side, the desert; on the other, a green meadow. With its sycamores it resembles from a distance a Norman plain with its apple-trees. The desert is a reddish-gray. Two of the Pyramids come into view, then a smaller one. To our left, Cairo appears, huddled on a hill; the dome of the mosque of Mohammed Ali; behind it, the bare Mokattam hills.

Arrival in Bulak, confusion of landing, a little less cudgeling than at Alexandria, however.

From Bulak to Cairo, rode along a kind of embankment planted with acacias or *gassis*.* We come into the Ezbekiyeh [Square], all landscaped. Trees, greenery. Take rooms at the Hôtel d'Orient.

* A kind of small palm. Bulak is Cairo's 'harbor' on the Nile.

III

First Days in Cairo

When we read in the following note that the travelers changed hotels, and when we see the name of one of the proprietors of the Hôtel du Nil, we cannot help thinking of Flaubert's total unawareness, at the time, of what the consequence was to be: the echoing of that name in the titles of two novels as yet unwritten—one, the first he was ever to publish: and the other, the last he was ever to write. Flaubert and Du Camp remained in the Hôtel du Nil throughout this first stay in Cairo (about two months) and returned there after their journey to Upper Egypt.

FROM FLAUBERT'S TRAVEL NOTES

. . . Night of our arrival in Cairo, feast-day of a *santon* [ascetic priest]: men drawn up in a rectangle, chanting, and making gestures as directed by a man at the center; another, in a corner, was singing the melody. The idiot face of a young man (skinny, thick-lipped, retreating forehead, beaked nose) caught by the giddy rhythm. A child singing too, twisting like the men.

Clowns at a wedding, one made up as a woman. Obscene jokes between patient and doctor: 'Who is it? No, I'll not let you in. Who is it?' 'It's . . .' 'No. Who? Who?' 'A whore.' 'Oh, do come in.' 'What's

the doctor doing?' 'He's in his garden.' 'Who with?'
'His donkey—he's buggering it.'

Yesterday, December 1, at the foot of the citadel,
we saw a mountebank with a boy of six or seven and
two barefoot little girls in blue smocks, their pointed
woolen caps on the ground beside them. The girls
were making imitation fart sounds with their hands.
The boy was excellent—short, ugly, stocky: 'If
you'll give me five paras I'll bring you my mother to
fuck. I wish you all kinds of prosperity, especially a
long prick.' The expression on his face as he said
'Allah!' on opening a jar filled with little cakes. The
Arab language had a charming sound. Two or three
carriages bearing pashas crossed the square, attracting
no attention. Threads of various colors hanging from
the mouth of the chief mountebank; double sticks
to beat himself with. In a deaf scene the boy, trying
desperately to make himself heard, shouted into the
chief's behind.

After a few days we leave the Hôtel d'Orient . . .
for the Hôtel du Nil, run by Bouvaret and Brochier—
fellow guests: Doctor Rüppel, Mourier, Delatour,
Baron Gottbert.* The upstairs hall is hung with
lithographs by Gavarni from the *Charivari*. When
sheiks from the Sinai come to do business with the
tourists, desert robes brush against all kinds of
things that civilization sends here as supposedly the
last word in Parisianism. (Bouvaret is a former provincial actor: he is responsible for the pictures);
prostitutes, Latin Quarter students, and Daumier's
bourgeois remain impassive as the negro goes by to
empty the chamberpots.

One day behind the Hôtel d'Orient we meet a

* Dr Rüppel was a German naturalist. The others are not
identified.

wedding procession. The drummers (small drums) are on donkey-back, richly dressed children on horses; women in black veils (seen full-face, the veils are like the paper disks that circus riders jump through, only black) uttering the *zagárit*;* a camel all covered with gold piastres; two naked wrestlers, oiled and wearing leather shorts, but not wrestling, just striking poses; men duelling with wooden swords and shields; a male dancer—it was Hasan el-Belbeissi—in drag, his hair braided on each side, embroidered jacket, eyebrows painted black, very ugly, gold piastres hanging down his back; around his body, as a belt, a chain of large square gold amulets; he clicks castanets; splendid writhings of belly and hips; he makes his belly undulate like waves; grand final bow with his trousers ballooning.

Soirée chez la Triestine. Little street behind the Hôtel d'Orient. We are taken upstairs into a large room. The divan projects out over the street; on both sides of the divan, small windows giving on the street, which cannot be shut. Opposite the divan, a large window without frame or glass; through it we see a palm-tree. On a large divan to the left, two women sitting cross-legged; on a kind of mantelpiece, a night-light and a bottle of raki. La Triestina comes down, a small woman, blonde, red-faced. The first of the two women—thick-lipped, snub nosed, gay, brutal. '*Un poco matta, Signor,*' said La Triestina; the second, large black eyes, straight nose, tired plaintive air, probably the mistress of some European

* 'Shrill, quavering cries of joy . . . produced by a sharp utterance of the voice, accompanied by a quick, tremulous motion of the tongue.' (Edward William Lane, *The Manners and Customs of the Modern Egyptians*, 1836.)

in Cairo. She understands two or three words of French and knows what the Cross of the Legion of Honor is. La Triestina was violently afraid of the police, begged us to make no noise. Abbas Pasha, who is fond only of men, makes things difficult for women; in this brothel it is forbidden to dance or play music. Nevertheless she played the *darabukeh* on the table with her fingers, while the other rolled her girdle, knotted it low on her hips, and danced; she did an Alexandrian dance which consists, as to arm movements, in raising the edge of each hand alternately to the forehead. Another dance: arms stretched out front, elbows a little bent, the torso motionless; the pelvis quivers. Preliminary ablutions of *ces dames*. A litter of kittens had to be removed from my bed. Hadely did not undo her jacket, making signs to show me she had a pain in her chest.

Effect: she in front of me, the rustle of her clothes, the sound made by the gold piastres of her snood—a clear, slow sound. Moonlight. She carried a torch.

On the matting: firm flesh, bronze arse, shaven cunt, dry though fatty; the whole thing gave the effect of a plague victim or a leperhouse. She helped me get back into my clothes. Her words in Arabic that I did not understand. They were questions of three or four words, and she waited for the answer; our eyes entered into each other's; the intensity of our gaze doubled. Joseph's expression amid all this. Love-making by interpreter.

In his letters Flaubert sometimes expands notes that he had made earlier. This is especially the case in his letters to Louis Bouilhet, which are the most detailed, most familiar, and most reflective. The description, in letters, with variations, of scenes already noted, is

3. Flaubert in Cairo, 1850. 'I would never allow anyone to photograph me. Max did it once, but I was in Nubian costume, standing, and seen from a considerable distance, in a garden.' (See p. 56.) The garden is that of the Hôtel du Nil, the name of one of whose proprietors, Bouvaret, Flaubert did not forget.

4. View of Cairo houses from a window of the Hôtel du Nil.

5. Eugène Delacroix: *Women of Algiers*. Evocative of Flaubert's '*Soirée chez la Triestine*' (see p. 39).

6. David Roberts, R.A.: *The Bazaar of the Silk Mercers, Cairo,* from *Egypt and Nubia* (1846).

7. The Sphinx. '"The Father of Terror" . . . no drawing that I have seen conveys a proper idea of it—best is an excellent photograph that Max has taken.' (See p. 50.)

8. A beach along the Nile.

9. Abu Simbel in 1850. 'Holy Thursday. We begin clearing operations, to disengage the chin of one of the exterior colossi.' (See p. 142.)

10. Temple of Kalabscheh: relief. Du Camp romantically captioned this figure 'Ptolémée Caesarion' (the son of Cleopatra and Julius Caesar): more probably it represents the Emperor Augustus.

usually an indication of Flaubert's particular interest in those experiences, and for that reason a few such repetitions have been included in the present text.

FLAUBERT TO LOUIS BOUILHET

Cairo, Saturday night, 10 o'clock
1 December 1849

Let me begin by giving you a great hug, holding my breath as long as possible, so that as I exhale onto this paper your spirit will be near me. I imagine that you must be thinking quite a bit about us. For we think quite a bit about you, and miss you a hundred times a day. Yesterday, for example, my dear sir, we were at the cat-house. But let's not jump ahead. At the present moment the moon is shining on the minarets—all is silence but for the occasional barking of dogs. My curtains are pulled back, and outside my window is the mass of the trees in the garden, black against the pale glimmer of the night. I am writing on a table with a green cloth, lit by two candles, and taking my ink from an ointment jar: near me, about ten millimeters away, are my ministerial instructions, which seem to be waiting impatiently for the day I'll use them as toilet paper. Behind the partition I hear the young Maxime, preparing solutions for his negatives. Upstairs sleep the mutes, namely Sassetti and the dragoman, the latter, if truth be known, one of the most arrant pimps, ruffians and old bardashes * that could ever be imagined. As for my lordship, I am wearing a large white cotton Nubian shirt, trimmed with little pompoms and of a cut whose description would take up too much space here. My head is completely shaved except for one lock at the occiput (by

* Bardash: a catamite (O.E.D.).

which Mohammed lifts you up on Judgment Day) and adorned with a tarboosh which is of a screaming red and made me half die of heat the first days I wore it. We look quite the pair of orientals—Max is especially marvellous when he smokes his *narghile* and fingers his beads. Considerations of safety limit our sartorial splurges: in Egypt the European is accorded greater respect than the native, so we won't dress up completely until we reach Syria.

And you, what are you up to in that wretched town that I sometimes surprise myself thinking of with affection? I keep thinking of our Sundays at Croisset when I would hear the sound of the iron gate and look up and see you with your notebook. When shall we be back chatting endlessly before the fire in my green armchairs? What of *Melaenis*? And the plays? Send me volumes. Until further notice write me to Cairo, and don't forget to put on the address: '*Chargé de mission en Orient*.'

. . . I am sure that as an intelligent man you don't expect me to send you an account of my trip . . . In a word, this is how I sum up my feelings so far: very little impressed by nature here—i.e. landscape, sky, desert (except the mirages); enormously excited by the cities and the people. Hugo would say that I was closer to God than to mankind. It probably comes of my having given more imagination and thought, before coming here, to things like horizon, greenery, sand, trees, sun, etc., than to houses, streets, costumes and faces. The result is that nature has been a re-discovery and the rest a discovery. There is one new element which I hadn't expected to see and which is tremendous here, and that is the grotesque. All the old comic business of the cudgeled slave, of the coarse trafficker in women, of the thieving merchant—it's all very fresh here, very genuine and charming. In the streets, in the houses, on any and all occasions, there is a merry proliferation of beatings right and left. There are guttural intonations that sound like the cries of wild beasts, and laughter, and flowing white robes, and ivory teeth flashing between thick lips, and flat negro noses, and dusty feet, and necklaces, and bracelets! Poor you! The pasha at Rosetta gave us a dinner at which there were ten negroes to serve us— they wore silk jackets and some had silver bracelets; and a little negro boy waved away the flies with a kind of feather-duster made of rushes. We ate with our fingers, the food was brought one dish at a time on a silver tray—about thirty different dishes made their appearance in this way. We were on divans in a wooden pavilion, windows open on the water. One of the finest things is the camel—I never tire of watching this strange beast that lurches like a turkey and sways its neck like a swan. Their cry is something that I wear myself out trying to imitate—I hope to bring it back with me—but it's hard to reproduce—a rattle with a kind of tremulous gargling as an accompaniment.

. . . The morning we arrived in Egypt . . . we had scarcely set foot on shore when Max, the old lecher, got excited over a negress who was drawing water at a fountain. He is just as excited by little negro boys. By whom is he *not* excited? Or, rather, by *what*? . . . Tomorrow we are to have a party on the river, with several whores dancing to the sound of *darabukehs* and castanets, their hair spangled with gold piastres. I'll try to make my next letter less disjointed—I've been interrupted twenty times in this one—and send you something worth while. The day before yesterday we were in the house of a woman who had two others there for us to lay. The place was dilapidated and open to all the winds and lit by a night-light—we could see a palm-tree through the unglassed window, and the two Turkish women wore silk robes embroidered with gold. This is a great place for contrasts: splendid things gleam in the dust. I performed on a mat that a family of cats had to be shooed off— a strange coitus, looking at each other without being able to exchange a word, and the exchange of looks is all the deeper for the curiosity and the surprise. My brain was too stimulated for me to enjoy it much otherwise. These shaved cunts make a strange effect—the flesh is hard as bronze, and my girl had a splendid arse.

Goodbye . . . Write to me, write to my mother sometimes . . .

4 December. Post scriptum. For you alone.
To amuse the crowd, Mohammed Ali's jester took a woman in a Cairo bazaar one day, set her on the counter of a shop, and coupled with her publicly while the shopkeeper calmly smoked his pipe.

On the road from Cairo to Shubra some time ago a young fellow had himself publicly buggered by a large monkey—as in the story above, to create a good opinion of himself and make people laugh.

A marabout died a while ago—an idiot—who had long passed as a saint marked by God; all the Moslem women came to see him and masturbated him—in the end he died of exhaustion—from morning to night it was a perpetual jacking-off. Oh Bouilhet, why weren't you that marabout ?

Quid dicis of the following fact: some time ago a *santon* (ascetic priest) used to walk through the streets of Cairo completely naked except for a cap on his head and another on his prick. To piss he would doff the prick-cap, and sterile women who wanted children would run up, put themselves under the parabola of his urine and rub themselves with it.

Goodbye—this morning I had a letter from my mother—she is very sad, poor thing. Talk to her about me.

Cairo, 2 December [1849]

Here we are in Cairo, my darling, where we shall probably stay the entire month of December, until the return of the pilgrims from Mecca, which should take place in a little more than three weeks. We are going to explore Cairo carefully and force ourselves to work every night, which we have not yet done. Towards the first of January we shall board a *cange**
and go up the Nile for six weeks, then drift down and return here. The entire journey to Upper Egypt is extremely easy and without the slightest danger of any kind, especially at this season when the heat is far from excessive. Therefore from now on you can change your opinion concerning the Egyptian climate. Mists come up after dark as they do anywhere else. The nights are cold (although the servants, or rather the slaves, sleep in the street, on the ground, outside the house doors), and there are clouds. To listen to some people in France, Egypt is a veritable oven: so it is, but it sometimes cools off. If you would like, darling, to have an inventory of what I wear these days (following the unanimous advice of sensible people

---

* Gallicization of the Arabic *gandja*, a Nile vessel with crossed sails. A more convenient word than *dahabieh*, also Arabic, which is commonly used in English.

here), this is how I dress: flannel body-belt, flannel shirt, flannel drawers, thick trousers, warm vest, thick neck-cloth, with an overcoat besides morning and evening; my head is shaved, and under my red tarboosh I wear two white skull-caps . . .

FROM FLAUBERT'S TRAVEL NOTES

Tuesday, 4 December. Good day. Coming back from the Hôtel d'Orient and looking for the workman who is repairing Maxime's tripod, I examined the pretty doorway of the building occupied by the Tuscan legation: romanesque arches with zigzag mouldings, shafts composed of four columns knotted like ropes; in the courtyard, two ostriches walking about freely, scratching fleas on their backs with their beaks.

Khan el-Kahlili—the goldsmith's bazaar—narrow, dark, noisy. Bazaar of the perfume-sellers. Back for lunch; four letters from my mother.

Ride to the Tombs of the Caliphs, between the rising ground beyond the gates of Cairo and the Mokattam. Gray color of the earth, tombs, mosques; on the horizon, in the direction of the Suez desert, hillocks like tents.

Mosque of X . . . (?) In the central court, a tree full of birds. We climb the minaret; the stones are worn, chipped. On the steps near the top, debris of birds, come there to die, the highest they could come, almost in the air. From there I have Cairo beneath me; to the right the desert, with camels gliding on it and their shadows beside them as escorts; opposite, beyond the plains and the Nile, the Pyramids. The Nile is dotted with white sails; the two large sails, crossed like a *fichu*, make the boat look like a flying swallow with two immense wings. The sky is completely blue, hawks wheel about us; below, far down, men are small, moving noiselessly. The liquid light seems to penetrate the surface of things and enter into them.

Maxime bargains with a woman for her coral necklace—necklace with silver-gilt ball. She was nursing a child; she hid herself to remove her necklace out of modesty, but she nevertheless showed both her '*tétons*,' as old Rüppel says. The transaction fell through.

At twilight, gray-blue-purple light pervades the atmosphere.

Back into the city—pipe and coffee at a café.

We begin our preparations for the expedition to the Pyramids. Everything satisfactory as regards physical health and morale: good spirits, good digestion. Remember: all is well.

IV

The Pyramids and Sakkara

It has sometimes been suggested by scholars that the very act of keeping a travel diary played a rôle in carrying the Romantic Flaubert towards Realism. Before accompanying him on the expedition to the Pyramids, readers might enjoy seeing how, as a young Romantic, he had written about the view from the top of the Great Pyramid only four years before, out of his imagination and his reading. So far as I know, this passage has never before been put into English: it is fairly typical of Flaubert's writings on the 'Orient' before his journey:

'When the traveler has reached the top of the pyramid, his hands are torn and his knees are bleeding; he is surrounded by the desert and devoured by the light, and the harsh air burns his lungs; utterly exhausted, and dazzled by the brilliance, he sinks down half dead on the stone, amidst the carcasses of birds come there to die. But lift your head! Look! Look! And you will see cities with domes of gold and minarets of porcelain, palaces of lava built on plinths of alabaster, marble-rimmed pools where sultanas come to bathe their bodies at the hour when the moon makes bluer the shadow of the groves and more limpid the silvery water of the fountains. Open your eyes! Open your eyes! Those arid mountains hide green valleys in their flanks, there are love songs in those bamboo huts, and in those old tombs sleep the still-crowned kings of olden times. You can hear the eagle scream in

the clouds; far off ring monastery bells; see the caravans setting out, the shells floating down-river; the forests grow vaster, the sea wider, the horizon more distant, touching the sky and becoming one with it. Look! Lend an ear, listen and look, O traveler! O thinker! And your thirst will be appeased, and all your life will have passed like a dream, for you will feel your soul go out toward the light and soar in the infinite.' (*From the first* Education Sentimentale.)

After that pantheistic rhapsody, here is the expedition as recorded in notes and letters:

FROM FLAUBERT'S TRAVEL NOTES

Departure. Friday [7 December 1849], set out at noon for the Pyramids.

Maxime is mounted on a white horse that keeps jerking its head, Sassetti on a small white horse, myself on a bay, Joseph on a donkey.

We pass Soliman Pasha's gardens. Island of Roda. We cross the Nile in a small boat: while our horses are being led aboard, a corpse in its coffin is borne past us. Energy of our oarsmen: they sing, shouting out the rhythm as they bend forward and back. The sail swells full and we skim along fast.

Gizeh. Mud houses as at 'Atfeh—palm grove. Two waterwheels, one turned by an ox and the other by a camel.

Now stretching out before us is an immense plain, very green, with squares of black soil which are the fields most recently plowed, the last from which the flood withdrew: they stand out like India ink on the solid green. I think of the invocation to Isis: 'Hail, hail, black soil of Egypt!' The soil of Egypt *is* black.

Some buffaloes are grazing, now and again a waterless muddy creek, in which our horses sink to their knees; soon we are crossing great puddles or creeks.

About half-past three we are almost on the edge of the desert, the three Pyramids looming up ahead of us. I can contain myself no longer, and dig in my spurs; my horse bursts into a gallop, splashing through the swamp. Two minutes later Maxime follows suit. Furious race. I begin to shout in spite of myself; we climb rapidly up to the Sphinx, clouds of sand swirling about us. At first our Arabs followed us, crying 'Sphinx! Sphinx! Oh! Oh! Oh!' It grew larger and larger, and rose out of the ground like a dog lifting itself up.

View of the Sphinx. Abu-el-Houl (Father of Terror). The sand, the Pyramids, the Sphinx, all gray and bathed in a great rosy light; the sky perfectly blue, eagles slowly wheeling and gliding around the tips of the Pyramids. We stop before the Sphinx; it fixes us with a terrifying stare; Maxime is quite pale; I am afraid of becoming giddy, and try to control my emotion. We ride off madly at full speed among the stones. We walk around the Pyramids, right at their feet. Our baggage is late in arriving; night falls.

Today the Sphinx is so familiar from photographs that the actual sight of it is apt to be an anti-climax, expecially when one finds it surrounded by touts and other tourist conveniences. But in those pre-photography days it must have been an amazing sight, enormously impressive. Flaubert wrote to Louis Bouilhet: 'No drawing that I have seen conveys a proper idea of it— best is an excellent photograph that Max has taken.' Du Camp, whose manuscript notes are generally very dry, says, about their confrontation with the monster: 'Gustave gives a loud cry, and I am pale, my legs trembling. I cannot remember ever having been moved so deeply.' And he wrote elsewhere: 'When we reached the Sphinx . . . Flaubert reined in his horse and cried, "I have seen the Sphinx fleeing toward Libya; it was galloping like a jackal." And he added: "That's from Saint Anthony."' As Flaubert wrote to Louis Bouilhet: 'We don't have emotions as po-hé-tiques as that every day, thank God; it would kill us.'

FROM FLAUBERT'S TRAVEL NOTES

The tent is raised. (That was its inauguration. Today, 27 June 1851, I have just folded it up with Bossière— very badly. This is its finis.) Dinner. Effect of the little white cloth lantern hanging from the tent-pole. Our guns are stacked. The Arabs sit in a circle around their fire or sleep wrapped in their blankets in the holes they have scooped in the sand; they lie there like corpses in their shrouds. I fall asleep in my pelisse, savoring all these things. The Arabs sing a monotonous *canzone*; I hear one telling a story. Desert life.

At two o'clock Joseph wakes us, thinking that day is breaking, but it was only a white cloud on the opposite horizon, and the Arabs had mistaken Sirius for Venus. I smoke a pipe in the starlight, looking up at the sky; a jackal howls.

Ascent. Up at five—the first—and wash in front of the tent in the canvas pail. We hear several jackals barking. Ascent of the Great Pyramid, the one to the right (Kheops). The stones, which at a distance of two hundred paces seem the size of paving-blocks, are in reality—the smallest of them—three feet high; generally they come up to our chests. We go up at the left hand corner (opposite the Pyramid of Khephren); the Arabs push and pull me; I am quickly exhausted, it is desperately tiring. I stop five or six times on the way up. Maxime started before me and goes fast. Finally I reach the top.

We wait a good half hour for the sunrise.

The sun was rising just opposite; the whole valley of the Nile, bathed in mist, seemed to be a still white sea; and the desert behind us, with its hillocks of sand, another ocean, deep purple, its waves all petrified. But as the sun climbed behind the Arabian chain the mist was torn into great shreds of filmy gauze; the meadows, cut by canals, were like green lawns with winding borders. To sum up: three colors— immense green at my feet in the foreground; the sky pale red—worn vermilion; behind and to the right, a rolling expanse looking scorched and iridescent, with the minarets of Cairo, *canges* passing in the distance, clusters of palms.

Finally the sky shows a streak of orange where the sun is about to rise. Everything between the horizon and us is all white and looks like an ocean; this recedes and lifts. The sun, it seems, is moving fast and climbing above oblong clouds that look like swan's down, of an inexpressible softness; the trees in the groves around the villages (Gizeh, Matariyeh, Bedrashein, etc.) seem to be in the sky itself, for the entire perspective is perpendicular, as I once saw it before, from the harbor of Picade in the Pyrenees; behind us, when we turn around, is the desert— purple waves of sand, a purple ocean.

The light increases. There are two things: the dry desert behind us, and before us an immense, delightful expanse of green, furrowed by endless canals, dotted here and there with tufts of palms; then, in the background, a little to the left, the minarets of Cairo and especially the mosque of Mohammed Ali (imitating Santa Sophia), towering above the others. (On the side of the Pyramid lit by the rising sun I see a business card: '*Humbert, Frotteur*' fastened to the stone. Pathetic condition of Maxime, who had raced up ahead of me to put it there; he nearly died of breathlessness.) Easy descent down the opposite face.

Interior of the Great Pyramid. After breakfast we visit the interior of the Pyramid. The opening is on the north. Smooth, even corridor (like a sewer), which you descend; then another corridor ascends; we slip on bat's dung. It seems that these corridors were made to allow the huge coffins to be drawn slowly into place. Before the king's chamber, wider corridors with great longitudinal grooves in the stone, as though a portcullis or something of the kind had been lowered there. King's chamber, all of granite in enormous blocks, empty sarcophagus at the far end. Queen's chamber, smaller, same square shape, probably communicating with the king's chamber.

As we emerge on hands and knees from one of the corridors, we meet a party of Englishmen who are coming in; they are in the same position as we; exchange of civilities; each party proceeds on its way.

Pyramid of Khephren. Nobody climbs it except Abdullah. 'Abdullah five minutes climb.' At the tip its [limestone] encrustation still exists, whitened by bird-droppings.

Interior. Belzoni's chamber. At the far end, an empty sarcophagus. In it Belzoni found only a few ox-bones—perhaps the bones of Apis. Under Belzoni's name, and no less large, is that of a M. Just de Chasseloup-Laubat. One is irritated by the number of imbeciles' names written everywhere: on the top of the Great Pyramid there is a certain Buffard, 79 Rue Saint-Martin, wallpaper-manufacturer, in black letters; an English fan of Jenny Lind's has written her name; there is also a pear, representing Louis-Philippe. (Almost all the names are modern.) Also scratched in the stone are little holes forming an Arab abacus; it's a game—pebbles are put in the holes for calculation.

Flaubert had read in Herodotus that the third Pyramid, today known as the Pyramid of Mykerinos, was built by order of Rhodopis, the Greek courtesan, and in his notes he preferred to give it her name. The ancient and the oriental courtesan were figures of glamor to the young Flaubert. In the first Education Sentimentale *he had written of his hero, Jules, that 'he adored the courtesan of antiquity as she came into the world on a day of bright sun, the beautiful and terrible woman who built pyramids with presents from her lovers; before her the rugs of Carthage were unrolled and Syrian tunics displayed; to her were sent amber from the land of the Sarmatians, feather-beds from the Caucasus, gold powder from the Senaar, coral from the Red Sea, diamonds from Golconda, gladiators from Thrace, ivory from the Indies, poets from Athens. The pale creature with eye of fire, the embracing, strangling viper of the Nile.'*

FROM FLAUBERT'S TRAVEL NOTES

Pyramid of Rhodopis. Inside, there are more bats than

in the others; their sharp little cry breaks the silence of these hidden dwellings. One chamber has collapsed: was it there that Rhodopis dwelt? The ceiling is made of two convex stones that meet, forming a very broad ogive.

... *Rock tomb behind the Great Pyramid*. On the walls, in low relief, priests, animal sacrifices, naval games; a cow calving; the calf is being pulled out by a man. The corridor is vaulted, but it is a single convex hollowed-out stone that forms the vault.

Sphinx. We sit on the sand smoking our pipes and staring at it. Its eyes still seem full of life; the left side is stained white by bird-droppings (the tip of the Pyramid of Khephren has the same long white stains); it exactly faces the rising sun, its head is gray, ears very large and protruding like a negro's, its neck is eroded; from the front it is seen in its entirety thanks to a great hollow dug in the sand; the fact that the nose is missing increases the flat, negroid effect. Besides, it was certainly Ethiopian; the lips are thick.

After we looked at the second Pyramid, our three Englishmen came to pay us a visit in our tent (we had invited them); coffee, *chibouks* [long pipes], fantasia staged by our Arab riders. Wriggling of the old sheik, his hands clasped on his stick. The Arabs crouch and jump up, clapping their hands and singing a Bedouin song meaning 'Round and round and round.'

We had hired a watchman from Gizeh, an imposing negro armed with a metal-tipped cudgel.

From the top of the Pyramid one of our guides pointed out the site of the battle, and said: '*Napouleoun*,

Sultan Kebir? *Aicouat, mameluks,*' and using both
hands he mimed the act of beheading.*

At night, strong wind; struck by great gusts, the
tent shudders and flaps like the sail of a ship.

Sunday. A cold morning, spent photographing; I
pose on tip of a pyramid—the one at the S.E. corner of
the Great Pyramid.†

In the afternoon we ride in the desert . . . We pass
between the first and second Pyramids and soon come
to a valley of sand, seemingly scooped out by a single
great gust of wind. Great expanses of stone that look
like lava. We gallop for a while, blowing our horns to
try them; silence. We have the impression that we
are on a beach and are about to see the sea; our
moustaches taste of salt, the wind is sharp and bracing,
footprints of jackals and camels half obliterated by the
wind. One keeps expecting to see something new from
the top of each hill, and each time it's only the desert.

We ride back; the sun is setting. Beyond, the green
Egypt; to the left, a slope that is entirely white, one
would swear it was snow; the foreground is all
purple—the small stones covering the ground glitter,
literally bathed in purple light; it is as though one
were looking at them through water so transparent as
to be invisible; coated with this light as though with
enamel, the gravel gleams with a metallic sheen. A
jackal runs up and disappears to the right: at this

* In the battle of the Pyramids, July 1st 1798, the gunfire of
Napoleon's troops mowed down the Mamelukes, who were
then finished off by saber.

† There is no trace of this photograph. Flaubert wrote later
to his mother: '. . . I would never allow anyone to photograph
me. Max did it once, but I was in Nubian costume, standing,
and seen from a considerable distance, in a garden.' (See
pp. 40–41.)

(56)

hour of nightfall one hears them barking. Back to the tent, skirting the base of the Pyramid of Khephren, which seems to me inordinately huge and completely sheer; it's like a cliff, like a thing of nature, a mountain —as though it had been created just as it is, and with something terrible about it, as if it were going to crush you. It is at sunset that the Pyramids must be seen.

Sunday, 9 December [1849]
8.30 p.m. Under the tent.

From the Pyramids to Memphis. Monday, 10
[December.]

We skirt the desert, which gradually diminishes and drops down into the valley. Sun, splendid air. The pyramids of Sakkara are much smaller and more ruinous than those of Gizeh. At Sakkara we lost our baggage; I wait in the center of the village (palm grove) while Maxime gallops through the surrounding countryside to find our men. A few Arabs were smoking beside an earthen wall. Courtyard enclosed by a palisade of dry reeds; chickens here and there. Our *saïs* [groom] in a short blue smock (he ran with his elbows held back, like a bird, his head forward) fastened by strings at the top, and wearing a little white turban, walked my sweating horse. Arabs show us the way and we reach Memphis. Camp on a kind of small promontory planted with palms, beside a large pond remaining from the flood; to the left, houses rising in terraces, with a white shrine; in the distance, flat perspective, verdure.

Tuesday morning, 11 [December]. Walk along the shore of the pond with our rifles over our shoulders . . . Pipe and coffee; we shoot some turtle-doves that are standing around the hole in which lies a colossus (Sesostris ?) flat on its face in the water; some of the birds are perched on the statue itself.

We mount our horses and ride across cultivated fields and down a long dusty path toward the pyramids of Sakkara. . . . Enormous number of scorpions. Arabs come up and offer us yellowed skulls and painted wooden panels. The soil seems to be composed of human debris; to adjust my horse's bridle my *saïs* took up a fragment of bone. The ground is pitted and mounded from diggings; everything is up and down; it would be dangerous to gallop over this treacherous plain. Camels pass, a black boy leading them.

To get some ibises we go down into a hole and then crawl along a passageway almost on our stomachs, inching over fine sand and fragments of pottery; at the far end the jars containing ibises are stacked like blocks of sugar at a grocer's, head to foot.

Rock tomb. [Mastaba of Ti.] Underground burial chamber. A narrow opening leads down through the sand: square, half-buried columns, remains of paintings and a very beautiful drawing: chambers vaulted with convex longitudinal stone blocks; modillions supporting the cornices, niches for mummies. It must have been a very beautiful place.

Return from Abusir to Memphis at a gallop.

We read our notes on Memphis, lying on the rug; fleas jump on the pages. Walk at sunset in the palm groves: their shadow stretches over the green of the crops, as columns must once have cast their shadows over now vanished pavements. The palm—an architectural tree. Everything in Egypt seems made for architecture—the planes of the fields, the vegetation, the human anatomy, the horizon lines.

Wednesday. Return to Cairo, riding under palms almost all the way. The dust around their feet is dappled with filtered sunlight; a field of flowering beans gives off fragrance; the sun is hot and good. I see a scarab under the feet of my horse. We cross the Nile at Bedrashein, leaving Tura, on the other bank, a bit to the right.

Large expanse of sand as far as the Tombs of the Mamelukes—good sun, the feeling of being on the road; dust, heat. I grip my horse with my knees and sit slouching, head down. We enter the city past the prison and the citadel.

Wednesday the 12th was my birthday—twenty-eight.

V

In Cairo

In Cairo, Du Camp had become an admirer of Charles Lambert (Lambert Bey), the Saint-Simonian, who was to have an influence on his subsequent career. Flaubert resisted Lambert's utilitarian doctrines, and in one of the last Egyptian notes we shall see him upholding against the Utilitarian the contrary doctrine of 'Art for Art's sake.' But Lambert was useful to the travelers.

FROM THE 'SOUVENIRS LITTÉRAIRES' OF MAXIME DU CAMP

Lambert had noticed that we were of inquiring mind and were not like idle tourists who travel simply in order to say they have traveled; he understood that what we wanted was to learn, and he helped us do so. He recommended to us an Arab named Khalil Effendi, who had had his training in France and was at that time tramping the pavements of Cairo looking unsuccessfully for work.

The story of this man is instructive, and will show how the regeneration of Egypt is being accomplished. He had been sent to Paris at the age of about twelve, at the expense of the Viceroy; he studied for a time in a *collège* and afterwards followed simultaneously the courses in the Polytechnic and the Law School; then he had been advised to go to Lyons, to learn silk-weaving and the silk business. When he returned to Cairo he was twenty-six, and had acquired much useful knowledge and many skills. At that moment Mohammed Ali, who had heard about the library at Alexandria burned by 'Amr ibn el-'As at the order of the Caliph Omar, had conceived the project of doing for Islam what the Alexandrians had done for antiquity, and filling the mosque of El-Azhar with all the books he could gather together. When he was told that Khalil, back from France, was looking for work, he appointed him chief binder at the library. Now Khalil Effendi had never trimmed a volume or handled a burnishing-iron. He declined the post he was offered. Mohammed Ali was furious, and said: 'He was in France, wasn't he? He should know how to do book-binding', and had him thrown out. Khalil, disgusted and starving, became a Protestant and a protégé of the British consul, who gave him a small stipend.

This man was relatively learned. He knew everything about the precepts of Islam, about Moslem customs, and about the cabalistic lore which is so thoroughly interwoven with religious ceremony as to form a part of the liturgy. We made an arrangement with him. For three francs an hour he was to spend four hours with us daily, answering our questions. It was money well earned and wisely spent. It was I who led the questioning, for I had the intention of using the information in a book to be called *Moslem Customs*. Birth, circumcision, marriage, the pilgrimage to Mecca, death-rites, and the last judgment, those six points, which in the Orient sum up almost the whole of life, were fully treated by Khalil Effendi, and we took notes as he spoke. I have just looked again at the thick notebook; my book is 'done'—what remains is to write it, and it will probably never be written. Flaubert intended to use his notes for an oriental tale he had in mind, and which he never wrote. Like so much other material gathered together, the result of Khalil Effendi's lectures has remained sterile; I have often regretted it; but I have never regretted those hours of work in our rooms at Cairo overlooking a garden of cassias, carob-trees and palms.

The result of Khalil Effendi's 'lectures' has so far continued to remain 'sterile.' Flaubert's sixty-three pages of notes were sold at auction in 1931, following the death of his niece, who had inherited them, and again in 1959; and their present whereabouts are unknown. Du Camp's notes, never printed, are in the Bibliothèque de l'Institut.

FROM FLAUBERT'S TRAVEL NOTES

Back in Cairo

Mosque of Sultan Hasan: round vestibule, pendentives or stalactites, great ropes hanging from high up. The slippers we put on are made of palm-leaves.

Mosque of El Kulum [El Keisun?], almost destroyed. Destined by Ibrahim Pasha to become a hospital but Abbas Pasha has taken away all the workmen for his country house on the Matariyeh road.

. . . On the Place Rumeileh we find our friends the mountebanks. The small boy was playing dead (doing it very well); a collection was taken up to resuscitate him. They put a metal *porte-mousqueton**

* The hook attached to an armed horseman's cross-belt, in which he rested the butt of his vertically-held rifle while riding. For the mountebanks it was an obscene '*objet trouvé*,' phallic in shape.

(62)

in his mouth and he walked around holding it there, quite naked. Not far off, a group of Arabs playing the *darabukeh* and singing; a little further, another was telling a story, incense burning near him.

Turkish bath. Little boy in red tarboosh who massaged my left thigh with a melancholy air.

Bride in the streets. I heard a wedding and hurried to see it. The bride, under a pink silk canopy, escorted by two women with magnificent eyes, especially the one on her left; the bride, as always, covered with a red veil, which with her conical head-dress makes her look like a column; she is so enmeshed she can scarcely walk.

About *santons*. A *santon* from Rosetta falls on a woman and fucks her publicly; the women present took off their veils and covered the copulation. Story of a Frenchman lost in Upper Egypt without resources; to live he has the idea of passing as a *santon*, and succeeds. Another Frenchman recognizes him. The '*santon*' ends up getting a 12,000-franc job with the army administration.

Sunday, 16 December 1849. As I went upstairs after lunch, I heard Mme —— 's shrill cries: she was dying. (On my divan I have been reading Bekir Bey's notes on Arabia; it is half-past three.) At three I went down to the garden to smoke a pipe. Mme —— was dead. From the stairs I heard her daughter's desperate weeping. Beside the pool, near the little monkey tied to the mimosa, was a Franciscan who greeted me; we exchanged glances; he said: '*Il y a encore un peu de verdoure*' and walked away. Children from the Jew's school were playing in the garden, two girls and three boys, of whom one was winding the squeaky spring of some toy soldiers. Dr Rüppel appeared and gave the monkey a nut; it jumped up on him and he cried: '*Ah cochon! Ah, cochon! Ah, petit cochon!*'; then he went off—to attend to business in the city, for he was wearing his hat. In the court-yard, Bouvaret, in his shirt-sleeves and smoking a cigar, told me: 'It's all over.' They'll be taking the mother away—and the daughter, who keeps clinging to her; now she is shrieking, almost barking.

She was an Englishwoman, brought up in Paris; in her neighbourhood she made the acquaintance of a young Moslem (now a *kaimmakam**) and was con-verted to his religion. The Moslem and the Catholic priests are wrangling about her burial; she made her confession this morning, but later she reverted to Mohammed and will be buried *à la Turque*.

Quarter to four.

Beginning Monday the 17th it rained all week—we spent our time analyzing Bekir Bey's notes and doing photography. Twice, wearing high boots, we ventured out into the Cairo streets, veritable lakes of mud; the poor shivering Arabs were wading in it halfway to their knees; business is suspended; the bazaars are closed, looking cold and dismal; houses are collapsing under the rain. To dry the mud, they scatter ashes and rubbish; thus the level of the soil gradually rises.

Saturday 22nd. Visit to the tomb of Ibrahim Pasha in the plain between the Mokattam and the Nile, beyond the prison. All the tombs of Mohammed Ali's family are in deplorable taste—rococo, Canova, Europo-Oriental, painted and festooned like cabarets, with little ballroom chandeliers.

* The Turkish governor of a small Egyptian province.

We walk along the aqueduct that supplies water to the citadel; stray dogs were sleeping and walking about in the sun, birds of prey wheeling in the sky. Dog tearing at the remains of a donkey—part of the skeleton, and the head, which was still completely covered with skin; the head is probably the worst part, because of the bones. Birds always begin with the eyes, and dogs usually with the stomach or the anus; they all go from the tenderest parts to the toughest.

Garden of Roda. Big, poorly maintained, full of fine trees, Indian palmetto. At the end, on the Cairo side, stairs going down to the water. Palace of Mohammed Bey (on the right as you face Cairo)—it was he who had a blacksmith nail horseshoes on the groom who asked him for new shoes. In the garden of Roda, close to a magnificent sycamore, a house that used to be rented to consuls; there one could really lead the oriental life.

. . . Kasr el-'Aini Hospital. Well maintained. The work of Clot Bey—his hand is still to be seen. Pretty cases of syphilis; in the ward of Abbas's Mamelukes, several have it in the arse. At a sign from the doctor, they all stood up on their beds, undid their trouser-belts (it was like army drill), and opened their anuses with their fingers to show their chancres. Enormous infundibula; one had a growth of hair inside his anus. One old man's prick entirely devoid of skin; I recoiled from the stench. A rachitic: hands curved backward, nails as long as claws; one could see the bone structure of his torso as clearly as a skeleton; the rest of his body, too, was fantastically thin, and his head was ringed with whitish leprosy.

Dissecting room: . . . On the table an Arab cadaver, wide open; beautiful black hair . . .

Monday 24 December [*1849*]. Spent the day in the Mokattam hills, where there was nothing to see. Lunch in a crevice between two rocks; the donkeys wander off and Joseph spends all his time looking for them. We walk in the desert, stretch out on the ground; not an idea, almost not a word; a pleasant day outdoors doing nothing ... We drank a cup of coffee in a café near the citadel and smoked long *sheeshehs* (water-pipes from Mecca). On my left, slightly behind me, a man had climbed onto a bench and was saying his prayers; a boy blew Joseph's horn as a joke; a donkey was at the door in a Parthenonian pose, one leg forward and its head held stiffly like Christ's donkey in Flandrin's fresco in St Germain des Prés. After saying his prayers, the man calmly combed his beard, as a gentleman might do in his *cabinet de toilette*. Maxime's donkey, which had been braying a good deal, finally made gargling sounds, like a camel—would it be because he had heard camels? The extent to which animals imitate others hasn't yet been studied: in the end it might denature their language, change their voices.

Midnight Mass (Latin). Bishop under a canopy, candles, columns decorated with red damask. Above, women's gallery in palmwood curving out like a belly (as though it couldn't help doing so, impelled by the feminine principle)—the veils of a few women could be glimpsed through it. While the priests were donning their chasubles, the organ played lilting tunes.

Tuesday, 25th. Christmas Day. Called on M. Delaporte. Mme Delaporte, petite, blonde, English; the lower part of her face makes me think of the Muse.*

* Delaporte was the French consul: 'the Muse,' Louise Colet.

Lambert is not at home. Mougel Bey. Interminable walk in the Ezbekiyeh with Lubbert and Bekir. These gentlemen live in perpetual dread of saying the wrong thing. What a stupid, dreary life! The son of the Sharif of Mecca with all his retinue, on horseback—cashmere turban, green *kaftan*, coffee complexion. Dinner: the conversation—at first light, to put it mildly, then socio-philosophical—can scarcely have been found entertaining by the company.

26 December. Visit to the mosques with Delatour* and Môsieu Malezieux; frock coat, high collar, hat, yellow gloves—pitiful fathead—utterly indifferent to Arab architecture. On the other hand, as we passed the negro slave market, near Bab el-Futuh, he livened up. 'I say, tell your guide to tell her to strip,' he said, pointing to a poor negress in front of us.

El-Azhar Mosque. In the court, mullahs on the ground in the sun, writing, discoursing; rows of columns—what one saw was circles of white turbans at the foot of columns. When the crowd pressed too close around us the sheik kept it back by hitting out with his stick. Brutality displayed by the guard from the consulate who was with us, to make people give us room to pass: on the steps of the mosques he took his long, silver-knobbed stick in both hands and struck out right and left.

Civilian Hospital of the Ezbekiyeh. Lunatics screaming in their cells. One old man weeping, begging to be beheaded. The black eunuch of the Grande Princesse came up and kissed my hands. One old woman begged me to fuck her—she uncovered her long, flat breasts

* Flaubert's mis-writing for Delaporte, the consul, perhaps (since a consular guard was present). Malezieux is unknown.

that hung down to her umbilicus and stroked them; she had an exquisitely sweet smile, her head bent to one side, lips parted over her teeth. Another woman, catching sight of me in the courtyard, began to do handsprings and show me her arse; she does this whenever she sees a man. A woman dancing in her cell, beating her tin chamberpot like a *darabukeh*.

. . . That night, 'masked ball' in a house in the street of the Rumanian whores. There were only two women in masks, looking like three-franc whores, wearing black jackets and furs. Large woman, the madam of the establishment; gaming table, bad drinks. A house that would like to show itself off but willy-nilly remains inconspicuous, like a thief in a crowd. Something comical about the stiffness and stupidity of it all.

Thursday, 27 [*December 1849*]. Bazaar of the perfume-sellers.* Visit to the Catholic bishop; refectory; those people eat well—two kinds of sponge-cake. Nothing to be gained there; after twenty minutes of conversation, almost entirely by me, I take my leave.

Tombs of the Caliphs, where Maxime takes pictures . . .

Friday, 28. Fruitless attempts to get commercial information. Visit to the Coptic bishop, who receives me in his courtyard† . . .

Saturday, 29 [*December 1849*]. At three in the afternoon, to the Polytechnic School at Bulak to pay our first call on Lambert Bey.

* There is a list of perfumes, oils and pomades at this point in the manuscript notebook.
† For this visit, see p. 72.

That night, an old man comes to see us. He knew Bonaparte and gives us an exact description of his appearance: 'Short, clean-shaven, the handsomest face he had ever seen, beautiful as a woman, with very yellow hair; he gave alms indiscriminately to Jews, Christians and Moslems.' Our old man told us that he is bored here and would like us to take him away to our country. He is an opium-smoker; the only effect it has on him is that he 'stays longer on top of his wife,' sometimes for an hour at a time. He was once very rich, has been married twenty-one times, and has lost all his money.

After our lunch on that same day we had dancers in —the famous Hasan el-Belbeissi and one other, with musicians; the second would have been noticed even without Hasan. They both wore the same costume— baggy trousers and embroidered jacket, their eyes painted with antimony (*kohl*). The jacket goes down to the abdomen, whereas the trousers, held by an enormous cashmere belt folded over several times, begin approximately at the pubis, so that the stomach, the small of the back and the beginning of the but-tocks are naked, seen through a bit of black gauze held in place by the upper and lower garments. The gauze ripples on the hips like a transparent wave with every movement they make. The shrilling of the flute and the pulsing of the *darabukeh* pierce one's very breast.

Here is a translation of what the singer sang during the dance:

'A slim-waisted Turkish object has sharp and piercing eyes.

'Because of them, the lovers have passed the night enchained like slaves.

'I am sacrificing my soul for the love of a doe capable of fettering lions.

'O God, how sweet it is to suck nectar from her mouth!

'Is that nectar not the cause of my languishment, my wasting away?

'O full moon, enough of harshness and of torment: high time you fulfilled the promise you made to the languishing lover.

'And, above all, make no end to the favors you grant him.'

The dancers move forward and back. Expressionlessness of their faces under the streaks of rouge and sweat.

The effect comes from the gravity of the face contrasted with the lascivious movements of the body; occasionally, one or the other lies down flat on his back like a woman about to offer herself, and then suddenly leaps up with a bound, like a tree straightening itself after a gust; then bows and curtseys; pauses; their red trousers suddenly puff out like oval balloons, then seem to collapse, expelling the air that has been swelling them. Now and again, during the dance, their impresario makes jokes and kisses Hasan on the belly. Hasan never for a moment stops watching himself in the mirror.

Meanwhile, Mourier was eating his lunch at a little round table on the left.

Sunday, [*30 December 1849*]. Visited the Coptic church in Old Cairo. As M. de Voltaire would have put it: 'A handful of rogues, gathered together in a hideous church, were celebrating with a total absence of style the rites of a religion whose very prayers they cannot comprehend.' From time to time one or another of the acolytes supplies, aloud, the pronunciation of some word the priest cannot read.

(70)

Crypt of the Virgin, where it is said she rested with her child on arriving in Egypt.

. . . Mosque of Amr, in Old Cairo, on the plan of the one in Mecca. We are shown the column that Omar whipped out of Mecca, ordering it to come here—which it did; one can see the mark of the whip. We are shown a well from which an Algerian recently drew up the cup he had dropped into the Well of Zemzem in Mecca. At the entrance, on the left, they show us a pair of twin columns; extremely close together though they are, a man who has never told a lie can pass between them, and then they move back together again.

FLAUBERT TO HIS MOTHER

Cairo, 5 January 1850

Your fine long letter of the 16th reached me as a New Year's present last Wednesday, dear old darling. I was paying an official call on our consul, when he was handed a large packet; he opened it immediately, and I seized the envelope that I recognized among a hundred others. (I was itching to open it, but manners, alas! forbade.) Fortunately, he showed us into his wife's salon, and as there was a letter for her too, from her mother, we gave each other mutual permission to read almost before saying how do you do. So you finally got my letters from Alexandria.

. . . I'm bursting to tell you my name. Do you know what the Arabs call me? Since they have great difficulty in pronouncing French names, they invent their own for us Franks. Can you guess? Abu-Chanab, which means 'Father of the Moustache.' That word, *abu*, father, is applied to everything connected with the chief detail that is being spoken about

—thus for merchants selling various commodities they say Father of the Shoes, Father of the Glue, Father of the Mustard, etc. Max's name is a very long one which I don't remember, and which means 'the man who is excessively thin.' Imagine my joy when I learned the honor being paid to that particular part of myself.

. . . Often when we have been out since early morning and feel hungry and don't want to take time to return to the hotel for lunch, we sit down in a Turkish restaurant. Here all the carving is done with one's hands, and everyone belches to his heart's content. Dining-room and kitchen are all one, and behind you at the great fireplace little pots bubble and steam under the eye of the chef in his white turban and rolled-up sleeves. I am careful to write down the names of all the dishes and their ingredients. Also, I have made a list of all the perfumes that are made in Cairo; it may be very useful to me somewhere. We have hired two dragomans. In the evening an Arab story-teller comes and reads us stories, and there is an effendi whom we pay to make translations for us.

. . . A few days ago I spent a fine afternoon. Max stayed at home to do I forget what, and I took Hasan (the second dragoman we have temporarily hired) and paid a visit to the bishop of the Copts for the sake of a conversation with him. I entered a square courtyard surrounded by columns, with a little garden in the middle—that is, a few big trees and a bed of dark greenery, around which ran a trellised wooden divan. My dragoman, with his wide trousers and his large-sleeved jacket, walked ahead; I behind. On one of the corners of the divan was sitting a scowling old personage with a long white beard, wearing an ample pelisse; books in a baroque kind of handwriting were strewn all about him. At a certain distance were standing three black-robed theologians, younger and also with long beards. The dragoman said: 'This is a French gentleman (*cawadja fransaoui*) who is traveling all over the world in search of knowledge, and who has come to you to speak of your religion.' Such is the kind of language they go in for here. Can you imagine how I talk to them? A while ago when I was looking at seeds in a shop a woman to whom I had given something said: 'Blessings on you, my sweet lord: God grant that you return safe and sound to your native land.' There is much use of such blessings and ritual formulas. When Max asked a groom if he wasn't tired, the answer was: 'The pleasure of being seen by you suffices.'

But to return to the bishop. He received me with many courtesies; coffee was brought, and soon I began to ask questions concerning the Trinity, the Virgin, the Gospels, the Eucharist—all my old erudition of *Saint Anthony* came back in a flood. It was superb, the sky blue above us, the trees, the books spread out, the old fellow ruminating in his beard before answering me, myself sitting cross-legged beside him, gesticulating with my pencil and taking notes, while Hasan stood motionless, translating aloud, and the three other theologians, sitting on stools, nodded their heads and interjected an occasional few words. I enjoyed it deeply. That was indeed the old Orient, land of religions and flowing robes. When the bishop gave out, one of the theologians replaced him; and when I finally saw that they were all somewhat flushed, I left. I am going back, for there is much to learn in that place. The Coptic religion is the most ancient of existing Christian sects, and little or nothing is known about it in Europe (so far as I know). I am going to talk with the Armenians, too, and the Greeks, and the Sunnites, and especially with Moslem scholars.

We are still waiting for the return of the caravan from Mecca; it is too good an event to miss, and we shall not leave for Upper Egypt until the pilgrims have arrived. There are some bizarre things to see, we have been told: priests' horses walking over prostrate bodies of the faithful, all kinds of dervishes, singers, etc.

. . . Max's days are entirely absorbed and consumed by photography. He is doing well, but grows desperate whenever he spoils a picture or finds that a plate has been badly washed. Really, if he doesn't take things easier he'll crack up. But he has been getting some superb results, and in consequence his spirits have been better the last few days. The day before yesterday a kicking mule almost smashed the entire equipment.

. . . When I think of my future (that happens rarely, for I generally think of nothing at all despite the elevated thoughts one should have in the presence of ruins!), when I ask myself: 'What shall I do when I return? What path shall I follow?' and the like, I am full of doubts and indecision. At every stage in my life I have shirked facing my problems in just this same way; and I shall die at eighty before having formed any opinion concerning myself or, perhaps, without writing anything that would have shown me what I could do. Is *Saint Anthony* good or bad? That is what I often ask myself, for example: who was mistaken, I or the others? However, I worry very little about any of this; I live like a plant, filling myself with sun and light, with colors and fresh air. I keep eating, so to speak; afterwards the digesting will have to be done, then the shitting; and the shit had better be good! That's the important thing.

... You ask me whether the Orient is up to what I imagined it to be. Yes, it is; and more than that, it extends far beyond the narrow idea I had of it. I have found, clearly delineated, everything that was hazy in my mind. Facts have taken the place of suppositions—so excellently so that it is often as though I were suddenly coming upon old forgotten dreams.

FROM FLAUBERT'S TRAVEL NOTES

Sunday, 6 January 1850. We spend all afternoon shooting birds of prey along Pharaoh's aqueduct. Whitish, wolf-like dogs with pointed ears frequent this malodorous region; they dig holes in the sand, nests where they lie. Carcasses of camels, horses, and donkeys. The muzzles of some of the dogs are purple with clotted blood that has been caked by the sun; bitches in whelp walk about with their big bellies; according to their nature they bark angrily or move aside to let us pass. A dog from another pack gets a far from friendly welcome here. Tiger-striped hoopoes with long beaks pick at the worms in the various corpses. A camel's ribs, flat and strong, look like curved palm-branches that have been stripped of their leaves. A caravan of fourteen camels passes along the arches of the aqueduct while I watch for vultures. The carrion stinks in the hot sun. The dogs doze as they digest, or tranquilly tear at the carrion.

After shooting at eagles and kites we took a few shots at the dogs; one bullet, landing near them, made them move off slowly, without running. We were on one hillock, they on another; all the hollow between us was in the shade. One white dog standing poised against the sun, ears erect. The one Maxime wounded in the shoulder half turned around, rolled on the ground in convulsions, then went off—probably to die in his hole. At the place where he was standing when hit, we saw a puddle of blood and a trail of drops leading in the direction of the slaughterhouse. The latter is a medium-sized enclosure about three hundred paces away; but there is a hundred times more carrion without than within, where there is little but entrails and a pool of filth. It is just beyond, between the wall and the hill behind it, that one generally sees the greatest number of wheeling circles of birds. All the land in this area is only mounds of ashes and broken pottery. On one piece of pottery, drops of blood.

It is along the aqueduct that one generally finds the soldiers' prostitutes, who let themselves be taken there in exchange for a few *paras*. During the shoot, Maxime disturbed a group of them, and I treated our three donkey-drivers to Venus at a price of sixty *paras* (one and a half piastres is about seven sous). That day, a few soldiers and women were smoking at the foot of the arches and eating oranges; one of them was keeping a look-out on top of the aqueduct. I shall never forget the brutal movement of my old donkey-driver as he came down on the girl, taking her in his right arm, caressing her breasts with his left hand, dragging her down, all in one movement, laughing with his great white teeth. His little black wooden *chibouk* attached to his back; the rags wrapped around the lower part of his diseased legs.

Monday, 7 January [1850]. Entry into Cairo of

Princess ——, mother-in-law of Abbas Pasha, returning from the pilgrimage to Mecca. We went to see the ceremony of her arrival at the palace, which is at the edge of the [Suez] desert. Pilgrims dismounting from their camels and throwing themselves into the arms of their friends or relations. Two men embrace in tears and then immediately go their separate ways. Desert maneuvers by the irregular infantry. Cold and very dusty; Bekir Bey invites us in with the staff; the band plays polkas. The bandmaster, huge paunch, in overcoat and high shoes, on horseback; Nubar Bey, a young Armenian with a Latin-Quarter air about him; the poor Turkish *pashas*, grotesque in their tight European uniforms.

The Princess's camels wear knee-pads decorated with pieces of mirror framed in rows of pearls; around their necks are triple bell-collars, and on their heads tufts of colored feathers. The windows of her litter are shaped like a ship's portholes and lined inside with mirrors. On the lances carried by the irregulars, the tips of the shafts are trimmed with bristles of feathers.

Wednesday, [*9 January 1850*]. I walk by myself in Cairo, in fine sunshine, in the section between the prison and the Bulak gate . . . I keep losing my way in the maze of alleys and running into dead-ends. From time to time I come on an open space with the debris of ruined houses, or rather with no houses; hens pecking, cats on walls. Quiet way of life here—intimate, secluded. Dazzling sun effects when one suddenly emerges from these alleys, so narrow that the roofs of the *moucharbiehs* [shuttered bay windows] on each side touch each other.

Thursday, 10. Re-entry of the caravan from Mecca.

Return of the —— Rug.* We get up early and stand in the street near the Bab el-Futuh to await the caravan. Women peering from windows under the eaves of the *moucharbiehs*—they veil themselves as soon as they notice they are being looked at.

Sitting on a camel, a man naked to the waist,

* This ceremony, which was called 'The Return of the Mahmal,' is described by Edward William Lane in his *The Manners and Customs of the Modern Egyptians*, a book which Flaubert, in one of his letters, urges his mother to read if she wants a detailed picture of his present surroundings. In a note Lane says: 'Almost all travelers have given erroneous accounts of the Mahmal; some asserting that its covering is that which is destined to be placed over the tomb of the Prophet; others, that it contains the covering which is to be suspended round the Kaabeh.' Flaubert was misinformed in that way: in his notebook he left a space blank for the name 'Mahmal,' which he apparently forgot, and then wrote the word '*tapis*'—'rug.' Actually the Mahmal was a kind of empty covered litter which traveled back and forth to Mecca each year on the back of 'a fine tall camel,' Lane says, 'which is generally indulged with exemption from every kind of labour during the remainder of its life.' Lane gives the legend behind it:

'It is related that the Sultan Ez-Zahir Beybars, King of Egypt, was the first who sent a Mahmal with the caravan of pilgrims to Mecca, in the year of the Flight 670 (A.D. 1272), or 675; but this custom, it is generally said, had its origin a few years before his succession to the throne. Sheger-ed-Durr (commonly called Shegeret-ed-Durr), a beautiful Turkish female slave, who became the favorite wife of the Sultan Es-Saleb Negm-ed-Deen, and on the death of his son (with whom terminated the dynasty of the house of Eiyoob) caused herself to be acknowledged as Queen of Egypt, performed the pilgrimage in a magnificent '*hodag*' (or covered litter), borne by a camel; and for several successive years her empty *hodag* was sent with the caravan merely for the sake of state. Hence, succeeding princes of Egypt sent, with each year's caravan of pilgrims, a kind of *hodag* (which received the name of 'Mahmal' or 'Mahmil'), as an emblem of royalty.'

Flaubert's 'man naked to the waist, swaying like a dervish,' may be the same so-called 'Sheik of the Camel' described by Lane as a well-known 'singular character,' who accompanied the Mahmal back and forth to Mecca every year, 'rolling his head during the whole of the journey.'

swaying rhythmically like a dervish. The men of the irregular cavalry—their bearing—superb in their rags and their ferocity—unpatched robes, dusty but not stained. Whereas the regulars, though well disciplined (comparatively), are in grotesque contrast—imitation of Europe—those poor officers, with their trouser straps under their shoes, and such shoes!

FLAUBERT TO DR JULES CLOQUET

Cairo, 15 January 1850

. . . So here we are in Egypt, 'land of the Pharaohs, land of the Ptolemies, land of Cleopatra' (as sublime stylists put it). Here we are and here we are living, our heads more hairless than our knees, smoking long pipes and drinking coffee on divans. What can I say about it all? What can I write you? As yet I am scarcely over the initial bedazzlement. It is like being hurled while still asleep into the midst of a Beethoven symphony, with the brasses at their most ear-splitting, the basses rumbling, and the flutes sighing away; each detail reaches out to grip you; it pinches you; and the more you concentrate on it the less you grasp the whole. Then gradually all this becomes harmonious and the pieces fall into place of themselves, in accordance with the laws of perspective. But the first days, by God, it is such a bewildering chaos of colours that your poor imagination is dazzled as though by continuous fireworks as you go about staring at minarets thick with white storks, at tired slaves stretched out in the sun on house terraces, at the patterns of sycamore branches against walls, with camel bells ringing in your ears and great herds of black goats bleating in the streets amid the horses and the donkeys and the pedlars. As soon as night falls, everyone goes about with his cloth lantern, and the pashas' grooms run through the city brandishing great lighted torches in their left hand. There is much jostling and arguing and fighting and rolling on the ground, much cursing of all kinds and shouting in all languages; the harsh Semitic syllables crack in the air like whiplashes. You brush against all the costumes of the Orient, elbow all its peoples (I speak now of Cairo); you see the Greek *papá* with his long beard riding his mule, the Albanian soldier in his embroidered jacket, the Copt in his black turban, the Persian in his fur pelisse, the desert Bedouin with his coffee-colored face walking gravely along enveloped in his white robes.

In Europe we picture the Arab as very serious. Here he is very merry, very artistic in gesticulation and ornamentation. Circumcisions and marriages seem to be nothing but pretexts for rejoicing and music-making. Those are the days when you hear the loud *zagárit* of the Arab women in the streets: swathed in veils and holding their elbows well out as they ride on their donkeys, they resemble nothing so much as black full-moons coming toward you on four-legged somethings. Officialdom is so far removed from the populace that the latter enjoys unlimited freedom—of speech, that is. The 'most extreme excesses of our Press' would give but a feeble idea of the buffooneries that are allowed in the public squares. Here the mountebank approaches the sublime in cynicism. If Boileau thought that Latin words offend chaste sensibilities, what on earth would he have said had he known Arabic! Furthermore, the Arab needs no dragoman to make himself understood: pantomime illustrates his comments. Even animals are made to participate in the obscene symbolism.

Anyone who is a little attentive *re*discovers here much more than he discovers. The seeds of a thousand notions that one carried within oneself grow and become more definite, like so many refreshed memories. Thus, as soon as I landed at Alexandria I saw before me, alive, the anatomy of the Egyptian sculptures: the high shoulders, long torso, thin legs, etc. The dances that we have had performed for us are of too hieratic a character not to have come from the dances of the old Orient, which is always young because nothing changes. Here the Bible is a picture of life today. Do you know that until a few years ago the murderer of an ox was still punished by death, exactly as in the time of Apis? You can see that there is much to enjoy in all this, and plenty of opportunity to utter stupidities about it—something which we abstain from as much as possible. If we were to publish anything it would be on our return. But between now and then, let nothing transpire. Lavallée had asked me for some articles or parts of my letters for the *Revue de l'Orient et d'Algérie.* He'll do without them, despite my promises, my firm intention being to *publish nothing* for a long time yet, for various reasons that I consider very serious and that I will explain to you later.

. . . It seems to me almost impossible that within a short time England won't become mistress of Egypt. She already keeps Aden full of her troops, the crossing of Suez will make it very easy for the redcoats to arrive in Cairo one fine morning—the news will reach France two weeks later and everyone will be very surprised! Remember my prediction: at the first sign of trouble in Europe, England will take Egypt, Russia will take Constantinople, and we, in retaliation, will get ourselves massacred in the mountains of Syria.

There is nothing here to halt an invasion; ten thousand men would be enough (French especially, because of the memory of Bonaparte, whom the Arabs regard almost as a demigod—the word is not too strong.) But it is not for us that the dough is being baked. The European employees will turn against the government here, which they detest, and all will be over. As for the Arab populace, it has no interest in knowing to whom it will belong. Under different names it will always remain the same, and will gain nothing because it has nothing to lose. Abbas Pasha—I whisper this in your ear—is a moron, almost a mental case, incapable of understanding anything or doing anything. He is undoing all the work of Mohammed Ali—the little that remains amounts to nothing. The general servility that prevails here (the baseness and cowardice) is nauseating—and on this score many of the Europeans are more oriental than the orientals . . .*

FLAUBERT TO LOUIS BOUILHET

Cairo, 15 January 1850

At noon today came your fine long letter that I was so hoping for. It moved me to the very guts and made a cry-baby of me. How constantly I think of you, you precious bastard! How many times a day I evoke you and miss you! . . . When next we see each other many days will have passed—I mean many things will have happened. Shall we still be the same, with nothing

* Anthony Trollope tells in his *Autobiography* that when he went to Egypt to reorganize the Post Office (in 1858) he found the worst corruption and obstructionism to be the work of 'an English heart and an English hand'—in that case an officer of the Peninsular and Oriental Steamship Company.

changed in the communion of our beings? I have too much pride in both of us not to think so. Carry on with your disgusting and sublime way of life, and then we'll see about beating those drums that we've long been keeping so tight. I am looking everywhere for something special to bring you. So far I have found nothing, except that in Memphis I cut two or three branches of palm for you to make into canes for yourself. I'm greatly giving myself over to the study of perfumes and to the composition of ointments. Yesterday I ate half a pastille so heating that for three hours I thought my tongue was on fire. I haunt the Turkish baths. I devoured the lines from *Melaenis*.* Come, let's be calm: no one incapable of restraint was ever a writer—at this moment I'm bursting—I'd like to let off steam and use you as a punching-bag— everything's mixed up and jostling everything else in my sick brain—let's try for some order. . . .

De Saltatoribus

We have not yet seen any dancing girls; they are all in exile in Upper Egypt. Good brothels no longer exist in Cairo, either. The party we were to have had on the Nile the last time I wrote you fell through—no loss there. But we have seen male dancers. Oh! Oh! Oh!

That was us, calling you. I was indignant and very sad that you were not here. Three or four musicians playing curious instruments (we'll bring some home) took up their positions at the end of the hotel dining room while one gentleman was still eating his lunch and the rest of us were sitting on the divan smoking our pipes. As dancers, imagine two rascals, quite ugly, but charming in their corruption, in their obscene

* Elsewhere in this letter, and in other letters to Bouilhet, Flaubert makes detailed suggestions for improvements in the lines from *Melaenis* that Bouilhet has sent him.

leerings and the femininity of their movements, dressed as women, their eyes painted with antimony. For costume, they had wide trousers . . .* From time to time, during the dance, the impresario, or pimp, who brought them plays around them, kissing them on the belly, the arse, and the small of the back, and making obscene remarks in an effort to put additional spice into a thing that is already quite clear in itself. It is too beautiful to be exciting. I doubt whether we shall find the women as good as the men; the ugliness of the latter adds greatly to the thing as art. I had a headache for the rest of the day, and I had to go and pee two or three times during the performance—a nervous reaction that I attribute particularly to the music.—I'll have this marvellous Hasan el-Belbeissi come again. He'll dance the Bee for me, in particular. Done by such a bardash as he, it can scarcely be a thing for babes.

Speaking of bardashes, this is what I know about them. Here it is quite accepted. One admits one's sodomy, and it is spoken of at table in the hotel. Sometimes you do a bit of denying, and then everybody teases you and you end up confessing. Traveling as we are for educational purposes, and charged with a mission by the government, we have considered it our duty to indulge in this form of ejaculation. So far the occasion has not presented itself. We continue to seek it, however. It's at the baths that such things take place. You reserve the bath for yourself (five francs including masseurs, pipe, coffee, sheet and towel) and you skewer your lad in one of the rooms. Be informed, furthermore, that all the bath-boys are bardashes. The final masseurs, the ones who come to

* There follows a description of Hasan el-Belbeissi and his partner closely resembling that in the travel notes.

rub you when all the rest is done, are usually quite nice young boys. We had our eye on one in an establishment very near our hotel. I reserved the bath exclusively for myself. I went, and the rascal was away that day! I was alone in the hot room, watching the daylight fade through the great circles of glass in the dome. Hot water was flowing everywhere; stretched out indolently I thought of a quantity of things as my pores tranquily dilated. It is very voluptuous and sweetly melancholy to take a bath like that quite alone, lost in those dim rooms where the slightest noise resounds like a cannon shot, while the naked *kellaas* call out to one another as they massage you, turning you over like embalmers preparing you for the tomb. That day (the day before yesterday, Monday) my *kellaa* was rubbing me gently, and when he came to the noble parts he lifted up my *boules d'amour* to clean them, then continuing to rub my chest with his left hand he began to pull with his right on my prick, and as he drew it up and down he leaned over my shoulder and said '*baksheesh, baksheesh.*' He was a man in his fifties, ignoble, disgusting—imagine the effect, and the word '*baksheesh, baksheesh.*' I pushed him away a little, saying '*làh, làh*' ('no, no')—he thought I was angry and took on a craven look—then I gave him a few pats on the shoulder, saying '*làh, làh*' again but more gently—he smiled a smile that meant, 'You're not fooling me—you like it as much as anybody, but today you've decided against it for some reason.' As for me, I laughed aloud like a dirty old man, and the shadowy vault of the bath echoed with the sound.

. . . A week ago I saw a monkey in the street jump on a donkey and try to jack him off—the donkey brayed and kicked, the monkey's owner shouted, the monkey itself squealed—apart from two or three children who laughed and me who found it very funny, no one paid any attention. When I described this to M. Belin, the secretary at the consulate, he told me of having seen an ostrich trying to violate a donkey. Max had himself jacked off the other day in a deserted section among some ruins and said it was very good.

Enough lubricities.

By means of *baksheesh* as always (*baksheesh* and the big stick are the essence of the Arab: you hear nothing else spoken of and see nothing else) we have been initiated into the fraternity of the *psylli*, or snake-charmers. We have had snakes put around our necks, around our hands, incantations have been recited over our heads, and our initiators have breathed into our mouths, all but inserting their tongues. It was great fun—the men who engage in such sinful enterprises practise their vile arts, as M. de Voltaire puts it, with singular competency.

. . . We speak with priests of all the religions. The people here sometimes assume really beautiful poses and attitudes. We have translations of songs, stories and traditions made for us—everything that is most folkloric and oriental. We employ scholars—literally. We look quite dashing and are quite insolent and permit ourselves great freedom of language—our hotel-keeper thinks we sometimes go a little far.

One of these days we're going to consult fortune-tellers—all part of our quest for the old ways of life here.

Dear fellow how I'd love to hug you—I'll be glad when I see your face again . . . Go and see my mother often—help her—write to her when she is away—the poor woman needs it. You'll be performing an act of the highest evangelism, and—psychologically—you'll witness the shy, gradual expansion of a fine and upright nature. Ah, you old bardash—if it weren't for her and for you I'd scarcely give a thought to home. At night when you are in your room and the lines don't come, and you're thinking of me, and bored, with your elbows on the table, take a sheet of paper and write me everything—I devoured your letter and have re-read it more than once. At this moment I have a vision of you in your shirt before the fire, feeling too warm, and contemplating your prick. By the way, write *cul* with an *l*— not *cu*: that shocked me . . .

FROM 'LE NIL, EGYPTE ET NUBIE' BY MAXIME DU CAMP[*]

Along with jugglers and acrobats must be mentioned the *psylli*, who are greatly feared in Cairo; snakes obey them, they can drive them away or attract them at will. Are they direct descendants of the *ophiogenes* of ancient Egypt? Have they learned by hereditary transmission the secret of the magicians who vied with Moses before Pharaoh's throne? Or are they merely very clever prestidigitators who play with snakes the way ours juggle disappearing balls? I know not.

I was curious to see them at close quarters, to watch their motions with unbiased eye, and, if possible, to ascertain their methods; I had them come to my hotel.

They appeared as a trio: an old man, a young man,

[*] In this book, published within a few years after the travelers' return to France, Du Camp nowhere mentions that Flaubert was with him.

and a boy of fifteen. They carried a knapsack that contained a squirming mass—several scorpions, two vipers, and a large black snake of a kind found in the Mokattam. The boy took the snake, wrapped it around his body, lifted it to his lips and let it glide several times between his shirt and his bare skin. He spat into its mouth, and pressed strongly with his thumb on the head of the innocent reptile, which immediately became as straight and stiff as a stick. This effect, surprising at first, is of course very easy to obtain. All one has to do is exert a violent pressure on the snake's brain (which is very weak), and thus induce a cataleptic state: the snake is immediately rendered immobile, so stiffened that it cannot be bent, only broken.

At my request the charmer entered my room, walked around it, and announced the presence of a viper. He undressed in front of me as proof that there would be no trickery, and striking the walls with a short stick he began to utter a sad, monotonous, slow whistle. Then he intoned a strange, imperious sort of incantation, only to break off and resume his whistling, but more softly than before. He said: 'In the name of clement and merciful God, I adjure you! I adjure you! If you are within, if you are without, show yourself! Show yourself! I adjure you in the name of one so great that I dare not say it! If it is your will to obey, appear! If it is your will to disobey, die! die! die!' Then he thrust his arms forward and undulated his body without shifting his place. He stood at the door of my room, and as I watched I saw a small grayish snake come out, moving quite fast across the shiny matting. The charmer caught it up and proudly showed it to me, asking at once for '*baksheesh kebir*'— 'a big tip.' The thing was well done, I admit, but it did not convince me: the young man who uttered the spells could very easily have taken advantage of a moment of distraction on my part and dropped into the room a snake that he had been concealing in his armpit all along.

The charmer then proposed to immunize me for the rest of my life against all kinds of bites, and to endow me with the power to handle with perfect safety all animals no matter how venomous. I accepted with pleasure, hoping for some kind of magical ceremony, and put myself in the boy's hands. I sat down cross-legged before him, he took my hand, pressed my thumb, wrapped a snake around my wrist, and addressed me in words that were rapid and staccato: he lifted the snake to my ear; it bit me hard; with a finger he took the blood from the bite and spread it on the ground; then he breathed twice into my mouth, made me breathe twice on the large black snake, which he had wrapped around my neck, twice rubbed my bloody ear with his hand that he had moistened with his saliva, once again asked me for 'a big tip'—and the thing was done. Very simple, as you see: not a very perilous initiation.

FROM FLAUBERT'S TRAVEL NOTES

[*Cairo*], *Thursday, 17 January* [*1850*]. Bulak, Nile, *cange*, sun; I inhale the vastness and the calm. To the baths—alone—the light through the circles of glass in the domes. Bardashes. Until one in the morning we work with Khalil Effendi.

This is Greek Epiphany—we go out at one in the morning. We sit in a café waiting for the church to open. Armenian church: a kind of glassed-in rotunda at the entrance, where candles are sold. As we enter, everyone is facing away from the altar, towards the door. The religious pictures are in the same style as those of the Copts. Lovely effect of the choruses at half-voice (sung by boys) which prolong the priest's long-drawn-out falsetto: when the falsetto finally fades away the choir picks it up *mezza voce*. Little beauty in the costumes. The sign of the cross is combined with real Moslem prostrations: first a sign of the cross, then a prostration with forehead touching the floor.

Another wait in the café: Max returns to the hotel and to bed, the Greeks not yet open. Third wait in the café: it is 4 a.m.

In the Greek church, Byzantine pictures in the Russian taste, making one think of snow. Entering the church for the second time, day was just beginning to dawn—I had that smartness of the eyes that comes from being up all night. Several upper-class Greek women came in. I was struck by a wave of pleasant fragrance that came out from under their veils, from the raising of their elbows when they reached up to be sure the veil was secure on their heads, and from the edges of the veils themselves as they floated up in a draft. In my mind's eye I still see a pink stocking, and the tip of a foot in a pointed yellow slipper.

The service was interminable. The Patriarch in his seat, looking haughty, and with a hard stare, several times reprimanded the women who were chatting in the gynaeceum. Small boy in overcoat going up to kiss his hand and prostrating himself. Too much hand-kissing. The Patriarch himself kisses the Gospel. After the collection, orange-flower water is poured over the hands of everyone present. I leave at eight and the Mass went on until ten!

Next morning, contract with Raïs Farghali at the consulate.*

FLAUBERT TO HIS MOTHER

Cairo, 18 January 1850

... We are waiting for the dervish ceremonies to begin and end before we set sail on the Nile. However, we shall look for a *cange* tomorrow morning. I'm going to go to Bulak to see a few. It is no slight matter. In any case, our faithful Joseph knows the captain (*raïs*) of a boat with whom he has already made the trip several times. Do you know how often this venerable dragoman has made this little excursion? About sixty times—he's a very intelligent fellow, and we couldn't be more satisfied with him. It's a blessing from heaven to have landed on such a man—most dragomans are appalling scoundrels. ...

THE SAME TO THE SAME

Cairo, 3 February 1850

... We shall leave for Upper Egypt as soon as Max gets the plates (for his photography) that he is expecting from Alexandria. Without that complication we'd have left this very afternoon. It will probably be next Wednesday. The evening of our departure we are to dine with Soliman Pasha. Our boat will be waiting at his water-gate, and if there is a wind we shall get off directly after dinner. We'll go up the

* This contract, for the rental of the *cange*, says that it belongs to 'Raïs Farghali Ibrahim,' and stipulates that there should be a crew of eleven, headed by 'Ibrahim Farghali, son of Farghali Ibrahim.' In Maxime Du Camp's 'The Crew of the Cange' (see Appendix), Farghali is called Ibrahim's uncle.

river as quickly as possible, stopping only when the wind stops—a thing that I gather happens quite often —and it is on our way back, downstream, that we shall stop and visit places at our leisure. The best thing is to go first to the farthest point, taking advantage of the weather. The return is always easy— you just let yourself drift with the current of the river, and if there's a little wind from the south you move along fast . . . We have letters of recommendation for all possible circumstances. You seem very worried about Persia; we have heard nothing about it yet. My darling, I renew the proposition I made to you last summer, before leaving. If, after Egypt—that is, next May—you feel that you have had enough, and can't go on, just say the word, and after seeing Syria and Palestine I'd come back by way of Constantinople and Athens, and you would see me in September (next) instead of the following February or March. Do as you like; I'll say nothing, not even to myself. But we're not at that point yet.

To return to the *cange*. It is painted blue; its *raïs* is called Ibrahim. There is a crew of nine. For quarters we have a room with two little divans facing each other, a large room with two beds, on one side of which there is a kind of alcove for our baggage and on the other an English-type head; and finally a third room where Sassetti will sleep and which will serve as store-room as well. The dragoman will sleep on deck. The latter is a gentleman who hasn't doffed his clothes a single time since we have had him; he is always dressed in toile and always saying '*Il fa trop chaud.*' His language is incredible and his appearance even more curious. However, he is a hearty and worthy kind of fellow, with whom one could go to the Antipodes without a scratch. As for young Sassetti, about whom you ask, we are not dissatisfied with him, even though he has taken a drop too much once or twice. I rather think that he is bored, or rather in not too good health, which comes from his absolute refusal to wear anything on his head. As for honesty, irreproachable.

. . . I think I caught my cold from standing for five hours on a wall watching the ceremony of the Doseh. Here is what it is. The word '*Doseh*' means 'Treading,' and never was name more properly bestowed, for what happens is that a man on horseback rides his mount over the backs of a number of other men stretched out on the ground like dogs. This celebration is repeated at certain times of the year, in Cairo only, in memory and as perpetuation of the miracle performed by a certain Moslem saint who rode his horse into Cairo over earthenware jars without breaking them. The *cadi* (sheik) who re-enacts this ceremony cannot hurt the prostrate men, just as the saint didn't break the jars. If the men die, it is due to their sins.

I saw dervishes who had iron spikes passed through their mouths and their chests, with oranges stuck on both ends of the spike. The crowd of the faithful was shouting with enthusiasm. Add to that, music wild enough to drive one crazy. When the sheik (the priest) on horseback appeared, the jolly crew lay down on the ground, heads to feet. They arranged themselves in a row like herrings, each one pressed close to the next so that there was not the slightest space between their bodies. A man walked over them, to make sure that this human plank would hold; and then, to drive back the crowd, a hail, a tempest, a hurricane, a veritable tornado of bastinados was rained right and left by the eunuchs on anyone who happened to be within reach. (We were up on a wall, Sassetti and Joseph just below us. We stayed there from eleven until nearly four. It was very cold, and there was scarcely room for us to move, the crowd was so dense and our perch so narrow. But it was excellent and we missed nothing.) We heard the thud of palmwood truncheons on tarbooshes, as though someone were clubbing bales of oakum or wool. That is exactly how it sounded. The sheik then advanced, his horse led by two grooms and he himself supported in the saddle by two others. The poor fellow needed them—his hands were beginning to shake, and he was clearly having an attack of nerves: by the end of his ride he was almost fainting. His horse walked slowly over the bodies of the more than two hundred men lying flat on the ground. It was impossible to learn anything about those who died as a result: the crowd pushed so close behind the sheik as he advanced that one could no more ascertain the fate of those poor wretches than learn what happens to a pin thrown into a river.*

Just the evening before, we had been in a monastery of dervishes where we saw one fall into convulsions from shouting 'Allah!' These are very fine sights, which would have brought many a good laugh from M. de Voltaire. Imagine his remarks about the poor old human mind! About fanaticism! Superstition! None of it made me laugh in the slightest, and it is all too *absorbing* to be appalling. The most terrible thing is their music.

* In his travel notebook Flaubert gives a few more details: 'The sharif in green turban, pale, black beard . . . The horse, dark chestnut, the sharif in green gloves . . . The horse advanced with long, exaggerated steps, and with repugnance, probably with nervous twitchings of the rump . . . Bekir Bey told us that no one was hurt.'

This is indeed a funny country. Yesterday, for example, we were at a café which is one of the best in Cairo, and where there were, at the same time as ourselves, inside, a donkey shitting and a gentleman who was pissing in a corner. No one finds that odd; no one says anything. Sometimes a man beside you will get up and begin to say his prayers, with great bowings and exclaimings, as though he were quite alone. No one even turns his head to look, it is all so natural. Can you imagine someone suddenly saying grace in the Café de Paris ?

The French consul-general arrived in Cairo recently. We saw him present his credentials to Abbas Pasha. It was a rather pathetic ceremony—the 'oriental splendor' was decidedly mediocre: for one thing, there was no 'splendor,' and the 'oriental color' was European and shabby at that. His Highness's Mamelukes were dressed like servants supplied by a caterer, and the coffee we were served was execrable. But the Viceroy's pipe was splendid—encrusted with enough diamonds to satisfy the lust of a hundred marquises. Nonetheless, and on the whole, it was exceedingly flat.

You speak about my mission. I have almost nothing to do, and I think that I will do almost nothing; and, such being the case, I should need considerably more cheek than I have to ask for compensation. I am becoming less and less covetous of anything at all. After my return I shall resume my good and splendid life of work, in my big study, in my comfortable armchairs, near you, my darling, and that will be all. So don't speak about pushing myself ahead. Push myself towards what ? What is there that can satisfy me except the voluptuous joy I always feel when I sit at my round table ? Haven't I everything that's most enviable in the world? Independence, the freedom of my fancy, my two hundred trimmed pens, and the art of using them. And then the Orient, especially Egypt, flattens out all the little worldly vanities. The sight of so many ruins destroys any desire to build shanties; all this ancient dust makes one indifferent to fame. At the present moment I see no reason whatever (even from a literary point of view) to do anything to get myself talked about. To live in Paris, to publish, to bestir myself—all that seems very tiresome, seen from this distance. Perhaps I shall have changed my mind in ten minutes. But I ask only one thing of kindred souls: to leave me alone, as I leave them.

... [*p.s.*] *5 February, 2 p.m.* Splendid weather— bright sun—and a good wind. We're off!

FROM FLAUBERT'S TRAVEL NOTES

Tuesday, 5 February [*1850*]. Dinner at Soliman Pasha's with M. Macherot, ex-professor of drawing at the school in Gizeh (abolished).

At eight o'clock, to bed in the *cange*. Devoured by fleas as a send-off.

VI

Up the
Nile to Wadi Halfa

Here I insert a few pages that I wrote on the Nile, on
board our *cange*. I had intended to write up my
journey in this way, paragraph by paragraph, in the
form of short chapters, whenever I had time; but that
proved unfeasible—I had to abandon the idea as soon
as the *khamsin* stopped and we could put our noses
outdoors. I had entitled it ' *The Cange*.'

THE CANGE

6 February 1850. . . . Today I am on the Nile and we
have just passed Memphis.

We left Old Cairo with a good north wind. Our
two sails, their angles intersecting, swelled to their
entire width, and the *cange* skimmed along, heeling,
its keel cutting the water. Sitting cross-legged in the
bow, our Raïs Ibrahim stared ahead, and from time to
time, without turning around, called back an order to
the crew. Standing on the poop that forms the roof
of our cabin, the mate held the tiller, smoking his
black wooden *chibouk*. The sun was bright, the sky

blue. With our glass we saw herons and storks here and there on the banks.

The water of the Nile is quite yellow; it carries a good deal of soil. One might think of it as being weary of all the countries it has crossed, weary of endlessly murmuring the same monotonous complaint that it has traveled too far. If the Niger and the Nile are but one and the same river, where does this water come from? What has it seen? Like the ocean, this river sends our thoughts back almost incalculable distances; then there is the eternal dream of Cleopatra, and the great memory of the sun, the golden sun of the Pharaohs. As evening fell, the sky turned all red to the right, all pink to the left. The pyramids of Sakkara stood out sharp and gray against the vermilion backdrop of the horizon. An incandescence glowed in all that part of the sky, drenching it with a golden light. On the other bank, to the left, everything was pink; the closer to the earth, the deeper the pink. The pink lifted and paled, becoming yellow, then greenish; then the green itself paled, and almost imperceptibly, through white, became the blue which made the vault above our heads, where there was the final melting of the transition (abrupt) between the two great colors.

Dance of the sailors. Joseph at his stoves. The boat heeling. The Nile in the middle of the landscape; and we in the middle of the Nile. Tufts of palm-trees grow at the base of the pyramids of Sakkara like nettles at the foot of graves.

Far away, on a river gentler and less ancient than this, I know a white house whose shutters are closed now that I am not there. The poplars, stripped of their leaves, are trembling in the cold mist, and cakes of ice are drifting on the river and being thrown up against the frozen banks. The cows are in their stable, the espaliers are covered with straw, and from the farm-house chimney smoke rises slowly into the gray sky.

I have left behind the long terrace, Louis XIV, bordered with lindens, where in summer I stroll in my white dressing-gown. In six weeks the trees will be budding, each branch will be studded with red. Then will come the primulas—yellow, green, pink, iris—decking the grass in the courts. Oh primulas, my pretty things, drop your seeds carefully, that I may see you another spring!

I have left behind the long wall hung with roses, and the summer-house beside the river. A mass of honeysuckle grows outside, climbing up over the wrought-iron balcony. At one o'clock in the morning, in July, by moonlight, it's a sweet place to fish for *caluyots*.

. . . So ends *The Cange*. Now I copy my notebooks.

FROM 'LE NIL, ÉGYPTE ET NUBIE'
BY MAXIME DU CAMP

. . . [Raïs Ibrahim] rarely conversed with the sailors, ate alone, and never smoked. For an Arab he was meticulously, almost elegantly, clean and neat, and despite the extreme simplicity of his costume, which consisted of a blue gown and white turban, he had a somehow lordly air which gave even greater distinction to his dark, animated features, his soft and con-templative eyes. One day when he removed his turban so that his head might be shaved, I saw his one lock of hair roll down to his waist—beautiful black hair that many women might have envied. He was harsh and haughty with his men, and sometimes struck

(99)

them, even drawing blood, but if it came to giving them an example in a difficult stretch of the river he would seize the oars or the poles and propel the boat himself.*

. . . The dragoman, Joseph Brichetti, was a singular individual of fifty-five, thin and alert, with a long grayish beard, eaten alive by a young woman he had recently married. He was a Genoese, and after a rather adventurous youth had sought his fortune in the Egyptian Army, in commerce, and in the service of travelers, without ever having been able to find it. He had arrived in Egypt, which he now knew almost to its tiniest village and its last palm. His language, a mixture of Arabic, French and Italian, was not easily understood . . . Before setting out on the Nile with Joseph, I sought information about him from a Frenchman who had employed him earlier; he answered with a long letter from which I quote the following sentence textually: 'Do-nothing, lazy and loafing—such are the vices of dragomans, especially drink and women.' I have to say that Joseph could not be reproached on any of those grounds; despite an unparalleled vanity he was assiduous and agreeable. His cleanliness, however, was more than doubtful: every morning, after having lightly passed over his eyes the slightly dampened corner of a towel, he would say with satisfaction: '*Ah, j'o fini mon tolette!*' In all the twenty-five years that the poor man had traveled in the Orient he had never been able to accustom himself to vermin. On the coast of Phoenicia, at Oum-Khaled-el-Moukhalid, where we camped at a spot which had recently been the stopping place of a caravan, I was awakened by Joseph's lamentations

* For more about Raïs Ibrahim and the rest of the crew, see Appendix, 'The Crew of the Cange.'

and found him scratching and moaning and crying out in desperation: '*Quo quantité de puces qui fa, bon Dieu!*' He could neither read nor write, an ignorance that caused him constant humiliation and regret. 'At this minute I would be a colonel with the Turks or captain of a Turkish frigate, if I knew how to write,' he told me one day, and I was convinced he was right. He was never drunk, robbed me not excessively, obeyed orders quickly, and was enormously useful on the Nile. He lived on fairly good terms with my servant, who in his quality of Frenchman despised all the 'savages' with whom he was now in contact. This latter was named Sassetti and had come with me from Paris. It is thanks to his intelligent help that I was able to bring to successful termination the photographic work that I had undertaken. He distilled the water and washed the utensils, leaving me free to devote myself to the fatiguing business of making negatives. If, some day, my soul is condemned to eternal damnation, it will be in punishment for the rage, the fury, the vexation of all kinds caused me by my photography, an art which at that time was far from being as easy and expeditious as it is today.

... Every time I visited a monument I had my photographic apparatus carried along and took with me one of my sailors, Hadji Ismael, an extremely handsome* Nubian, whom I had climb up on to the ruins which I wanted to photograph. In this way I was always able to include a uniform scale of proportions. The great difficulty was to get Hadji Ismael to stand perfectly motionless while I performed my operations;

* '*Fort beau.*' But see p. 224. Perhaps Du Camp means 'well built.'

and I finally succeeded by means of a trick whose success will convey the depth of naiveté of these poor Arabs. I told him that the brass tube of the lens jutting from the camera was a cannon, which would vomit a hail of shot if he had the misfortune to move—a story which immobilized him completely, as can be seen from my plates.

The day I was returning from Dendera I overheard the following conversation between him and Raïs Ibrahim—a curious account of a photographic expedition:

'Well, Hadji Ismael, what news?' asked the *raïs* as we boarded the *cange*.

'None,' the sailor answered. 'The Father of Thinness ('Abu Muknaf,' as I was always called by my crew) ordered me to climb up on a column that bore the huge face of an idol; he wrapped his head in the black veil, he turned his yellow cannon towards me, then he cried: "Do not move!" The cannon looked at me with its little shining eye, but I kept very still, and it did not kill me.'

'God is the greatest,' said Raïs Ibrahim, sententiously.

'And our Lord Mohammed is his prophet,' replied Hadji.

... [According to Mohammedan Law], full and complete ablution is indispensable following certain bodily acts. When a husband leaves the women's appartments, for example, he must entirely submerge himself—in a pool, in a river, anywhere, so long as his head is momentarily under water. When he emerges, he raises his hands to heaven and says: 'O Lord, I render thee thanks for the joys thou hast given me, and I pray thee to lead in holy ways the child that may be born. O my God, make me blind in the presence of unlawful women!'

Very often, standing on my *cange* at daybreak, I have seen fellahin run to the Nile, strip off their clothing, and plunge into the river. At such moments my sailors would laugh and call out to the bathers pleasantries which were, to put it mildly, indelicate.

FROM FLAUBERT'S TRAVEL NOTES

Thursday morning, 7 [February 1850]. When I come on deck, we are very close to the shore. The color of the earth is exactly that of the Nubian women I saw in the slave market.

Khamsin. We shut ourselves in; sand grits between our teeth and makes our faces unrecognizable; it gets into our tin boxes and spoils our supplies—cooking is impossible ... Great whirlwinds of sand rise up and beat against the sides of our *cange*; everyone takes to his bed. A *cange* carrying a party of Englishmen comes sailing furiously down the river, spinning in the wind. ...

FROM 'LE NIL, EGYPTE ET NUBIE,' BY MAXIME DU CAMP

Here they call this wind the *khamsin* (fifty), because it usually blows for fifty days. It is an ocean of dust borne by a hurricane; the sky turns a leaden gray, and the sun, behind a dark veil and shorn of its rays, looks like a great shield of dull rilver. The sand, whirled about by the wind, covers everything and penetrates everything. At Philae, after a *khamsin* whirlwind, I found a powdering of sand even in the springs of my watch, which was inside a double case in a buttoned-down pocket.

FROM FLAUBERT'S TRAVEL NOTES

Friday, [*8 February 1850*]. Towing by rope this morning for four hours . . .

Monday, [*11 February 1850*]. . . . Golden clouds, like satin sofas. The sky is full of bluish, pigeon's-breast tints: the sun is setting in the desert. To the left, the Arabian chain with its indentations; it is flat on top, a plateau, in the foreground, palms, and this foreground is bathed in darkness; in the middle ground, beyond the palms, camels pass, and two or three Arabs riding donkeys. What silence! Not a sound. Two great strips of sand, and the sun! One sees how awesome it might be here. The Sphinx has something of the same effect.

FROM 'LE NIL, EGYPTE ET NUBIE' BY MAXIME DU CAMP

Navigation on the Nile takes on oceanic proportions not to be found on any of the rivers of our cold countries. When the wind blows, we unfurl the enormous triangular sails, which strain from the masts; one hears the wake of the boat, the sailors are happy, they sing, tell each other stories full of marvels, or sleep on their mats in the strip of shade beside the bulwarks. In a calm, or against a head wind, if the water is not too deep we keep the boat going with the help of long poles: the man closest to the bow, who can be in an almost prostrate position at the end of a long push, intones a kind of litany to which the others respond; and they will sometimes keep that up all day, chanting their monotonous refrain, interspersing it with shouts of self-encouragement, dripping with sweat from the fatigue of this brutal work. When the river is high and the poles do not touch bottom, the sailors dive in, a rope between their teeth; they line up on the bank, harness themselves to the long cable attached to the ship's mast, and pull the *cange* ahead like so many draft horses. In this way a slight progress is made against the current and the wind. I would take advantage of these painful, slow processions to go ashore with one of the sailors and my rifle, and do some shooting in the countryside.

FLAUBERT TO HIS MOTHER

[written before reaching Benisuef on 13 February 1850]

. . . We are leading a good life, my dear old darling. Oh, how sorry I am that you are not here! How you would love it! If you knew what calm surrounds us, and how peaceful are the depths we feel our minds explore—we laze, we loaf, we daydream. In the morning I study Greek, read Homer, in the afternoon I write. During the day we often take our rifles and look for game. I'm getting quite good, much to my amusement—me, a good shot! You'll think me a bragging child when I tell you that last Saturday we killed 54 pieces of game, all doves or pigeons: they perch in the palms and one has only to pick them off. We live on what we shoot. Joseph gives himself up to his passion for cooking and makes us such stews as he can, but he is beginning to think that we have had enough pigeons and doves. He is right—we have been living on nothing else. Tonight let's hope we may get some beef for the next few days. Our only drink is water, and we eat a lot of preserves, dates, oranges, figs and other light fare. I am growing ignobly fat. Sassetti is getting to be a balloon: only Max stays thin. Our mattresses, or rather our mattress, is of the thickness of a blanket, and our blanket is like a woolen stocking. We sleep none the worse for that—sometimes fifteen hours at a stretch.

At this moment, one o'clock in the afternoon, Max is stretched out on my right on his bed, reading. I am sitting on a folding chair, writing this on my knee, in the room we share. On the board that serves as my bed (we take it up every morning and put it back at night) and which we use as a table during the day, my things are spread out, and a little further off there are two glasses of excellent lemonade . . .

With the cange *tied up at Benisuef, the two travelers made a four-day excursion to the oasis of the Fayum and to the Birket Karun, the inland sea that is the remains of the much larger ancient lake Moeris, about which their curiosity had been aroused by Herodotus. They spent two nights 'sleeping on mats on the ground and living exactly like Arabs—except for the fleas all was well,' as Flaubert wrote to his mother a week later; and then two nights in the town of Medinet el-Fayum. There, finding the guest-rooms of a Christian monastery where Max had counted on staying already occupied by a party of German naturalists—Flaubert sketched the interlopers in his notes as 'trouserless, but wearing overcoats, and sniffing* raki'—*they were taken in by a hospitable, well-to-do Christian farmer who was 'quite learned in religious matters. We talked (with Joseph's help, of course) about St Anthony (we were in St Anthony's country), about Arius, about St Athanasius. It was marvelous.' In that same letter to his mother, written when he was back on the* cange *continuing the voyage up the Nile, he asserted himself about something she had brought up in her last letter:*

FLAUBERT TO HIS MOTHER

Between Minia and Assiut
23 February 1850

... Now I come to something that you seem to enjoy reverting to and that I fail completely to understand. You are never at a loss for things to torment yourself about. What is the sense of this: that I must have a job—'a small job,' you say. First of all, *what* job? I defy you to find me one, to specify in what field, what it would consist in. Frankly, and without deluding yourself, is there a single one that I am capable of filling? You add: 'One that wouldn't take up much of your time and wouldn't prevent you from doing other things.' There's the delusion! That's what Bouilhet told himself when he took up medicine, what I told myself when I began law, which only just failed to kill me with bottled-up fury. When one does something, one must do it wholly and well. Those bastard existences where you sell suet all day and write poetry at night are made for mediocre minds— like those horses that are equally good for saddle and carriage, the worst kind, that can neither jump a ditch nor pull a plow.

In short, it seems to me that one takes a job for money, for honors, or as an escape from idleness. Now you'll grant me, darling, (1) that I keep busy enough not to have to go out looking for something to do; and (2) if it's a question of honors, my vanity is such that I'm incapable of feeling myself honored by anything:

a position, however high it might be (and that isn't the kind you speak of) will never give me the satisfaction that I derive from my self-respect when I have accomplished something well in my own way, and finally, if it's for money, any jobs or job that I could have would bring in too little to make much difference to my income. Weigh all those considerations: *don't knock your head against a hollow idea.* Is there any position in which I'd be closer to you, more yours? And isn't not to be bored one of the principal goals of life?

Flaubert's reminder to his mother that his having no job would keep him close to her was effective: there are no further suggestions that he seek 'une petite place.'

FROM 'LE NIL, EGYPTE ET NUBIE' BY MAXIME DU CAMP

One evening the wind suddenly died, stopping us beside a great sycamore, beyond which I could just make out, in the last faint light of day, a few houses and the minaret of a small mosque. It was the village of Sheikh 'Abadeh. The next morning as dawn was breaking I went to see it, for it was here that once stood the city of Antinoöpolis, which Hadrian built on the site of the ancient Besa. Antinous had drowned himself in the Nile: he was proclaimed a god, and a city was built, full of temples where incense burned in his honor.

Among the mud houses, beneath magnificent palms, there are heaps of smashed and mutilated ruins, brick domes that had been parts of baths, an overturned votive altar, a colonnade still standing but decapitated, the stumps of a triumphal arch, composite capitals in Ethiopian stone, hollowed-out pillars put to use as mortars, mounds of debris; all of it sad, gray, desolate amid the dust. And yet only twenty years ago there wĕre three well-preserved Roman temples here, an entire portico, a triumphal arch so lofty that the palm-trees rested their fruit-laden heads against it, and the marble basins of sunken baths—in fact the monumental city remained intact. But one day Ibrahim Pasha decided to build sugar refineries on the opposite bank, near Roda; he laid his predatory hands on the Roman buildings, tore them down, and used the stones for the construction of a hideous factory.

. . . On February 26 our boat anchored at Assiut, capital of Upper Egypt. According to my contract with Raïs Ibrahim, I was to let him spend twenty-four hours at Assiut and the same at Esna, in order that he might renew the supply of biscuits for his crew . . . Assiut is the place of rendezvous for caravans coming from Darfur. Here thcy arrive exhausted, depleted by the fatigues and privations of the journey, dragging their bands of slaves and parched by the heat of the desert. Here they stop for quarantine—a compulsory rest, which the *gellabs* (slave traders) take advantage of to mutilate their young negroes, fitting them for service in the harems.

FROM FLAUBERT'S TRAVEL NOTES

Assiut. [*26 February 1850*]. . . . We climb up to the rock-tombs of old Lycopolis . . . Our guide takes us by the hand and leads us with an air of mystery—to show us the print of a woman's shoe in the sand!

She was an Englishwoman, there a few days ago. Poor fellow!*

... At twilight we return to the *cange*; the people walking on the riverbank look like shadows thrown on a screen. Night falls.

Assiut. Wednesday [*27 February 1850*]. Our grotesque, Schimi, has deserted. After waiting a while for him, we leave at eleven o'clock.

Kena. Sunday morning, [*3 March 1850*]. ... The bazaars smell of coffee and sandalwood. At the bend of one of the streets, to the right as you leave the bazaar, we suddenly find ourselves in the quarter of the *almehs* [prostitutes]. The street curves a little; the houses, of gray earth, are no more than four feet high. To the left, sloping down toward the Nile, another street and a palm-tree. Blue sky. The women are sitting in their doorways on mats, or standing. Light-colored robes, one over the other, hang loosely in the hot wind; blue robes around the bodies of the negresses. The clothes are sky-blue, bright yellow, pink, red—all contrasting with the differently-colored skins. Necklaces of gold piastres falling to their knees; on their heads, piastres threaded on silk and attached to the ends of the hair—they tinkle. The negresses have vertical knife-marks on their cheeks, usually three on each cheek: this is done in infancy, with a red-hot knife.

Fat woman (Mme Maurice) in blue, deep-set dark eyes, square chin, small hands, eyebrows heavily

* Du Camp, in *Le Nil*, puts the dot on the i by adding to his mention of this little episode the fact that the guide said 'with a great sigh: "I'll see her again when she comes back from Upper Egypt."'

(110)

painted, pleasant-looking. Girl with frizzy hair brought down over her forehead, slightly marked by smallpox (in the street that continues the bazaar, going straight ahead to Bir 'Ambar, past the Greek grocery). Another was wearing a striped Syrian *habar* [hooded robe]. Tall girl with such a soft voice, calling '*Cawadja! Cawadja!*' The sun was very strong.

Inopportune arrival of Fioravi (M. de Lauture told me that he has since died) and Ortalli: no escaping going to their house.

. . . We return to the street of the *almehs*. I walk along it deliberately: they call out to me: '*Cawadja, cawadja, baksheesh! Baksheesh! Cawadja!*' I give some of them a few piastres; a few put their arms around me and try to pull me inside: I deliberately abstain from going with them, lest it spoil the sweet sadness of it all, and I walk away.

. . . We have a new sailor, Mansur.

. . . At night a few stars are reflected in the water, elongated there like the flames of great torches. During the day, in the sun, a diamond star glitters at the tip of each wave.

Monday, 4 March. . . . We have passed Luxor. I was cleaning my glass when we sighted Luxor on the left: I climbed on to the roof of the cabin. The seven columns, the obelisk, the French House, Arabs sitting beside the water near an English *cange*. The caretaker of the French House calls out that he has a letter for us . . . We stop. Among the people at the landing a negro, swathed like a mummy— all cartilage, desiccated, with a small, dirty *takieh* [cap] on the top of his head; women are bathing their feet in the river, a donkey has come down to drink.

Sunset over Medinet Habu. The mountains are dark indigo (on the Medinet Habu side); blue over dark gray, with contrasting horizontal stripes of purplish red in the clefts of the valleys. The palms are black as ink, the sky is red, the Nile has the look of a lake of molten steel.

When we arrived off Thebes our sailors were drumming on their *darabukehs*, the mate was playing his flute, Khalil was dancing with his castanets: they broke off to land.

It was then, as I was enjoying those things, and just as I was watching three wave-crests bending under the wind behind us, that I felt a surge of solemn happiness that reached out towards what I was seeing, and I thanked God in my heart for having made me capable of such a joy: I felt fortunate at the thought, and yet it seemed to me that I was thinking of nothing: it was a sensuous pleasure that pervaded my entire being.*

When Flaubert wrote to Louis Bouilhet from Cairo on January 15th: 'We have not yet seen any dancing girls; they are all in exile in Upper Egypt. Good brothels no longer exist in Cairo either,' he was referring to an 1834 edict by Mohammed Ali that had prohibited female dancing and prostitution in Cairo and ordered the deportation of all known 'courtesans' to three cities—Kena, Esna and Assuan. The name almehs (said to come from the Arabic awaleim, 'learned women') had originally signified

* That beautiful passage was slightly changed by Flaubert from the original notebook entry, which reads: '*Considérant tout cela, et jouissant de le considérer, à un moment où je regardais trois plis de vagues qui se courbaient derrière nous, sous le vent, j'ai senti un mouvement religieux dans mon moi et j'ai remercié Dieu de m'avoir fait apte à jouir de cette manière. Je me suis senti heureux par la pensée, quoiqu'il me semblait alors ne penser à rien.*'

professional women improvisers of songs and poems, but had come to be applied to all female entertainers, and in 1850 meant little more than dancing girls, all of whom were prostitutes as well. Among them Kuchuk Hanem, at Esna, was a star, of whom the travelers had undoubtedly heard in Cairo. Her Turkish name is said to mean either 'Pretty Little Princess' or simply 'Dancing Woman.'

FROM FLAUBERT'S TRAVEL NOTES

Esna. Wednesday, 6 March 1850. Reached Esna about nine in the morning.

. . . *Bambeh.* While we were breakfasting, an *almeh* came to speak with Joseph, She was thin, with a narrow forehead, her eyes painted with antimony, a veil passed over her head and held by her elbows. She was followed by a pet sheep, whose wool was painted in spots with yellow henna. Around its nose was a black velvet muzzle. It was very wooly, its feet like those of a toy sheep, and it never left its mistress.

We go ashore. The town is like all the others, built of dried mud, smaller than Kena; the bazaars less rich. On the square, Albanian soldiers at a café. The postal authorities 'reside' on the square: that is, the effendi comes there to perform his functions. School above a mosque, where we go to buy some ink. First visit to the temple, where we stay but a moment. The houses have a kind of square tower, with poles thick with pigeons. In the doorways, a few *almehs*, fewer than at Kena, their dress less brilliant and their aspect less bold.

House of Kuchuk Hanem. Bambeh precedes us, accompanied by her sheep; she pushes open a door and we enter a house with a small courtyard and a stairway opposite the door. On the stairs, opposite us, surrounded by light and standing against the background of blue sky, a woman in pink trousers. Above, she wore only dark violet gauze.

She had just come from the bath, her firm breasts had a fresh smell, something like that of sweetened turpentine; she began by perfuming her hands with rose water.

We went up to the first floor. Turning to the left at the top of the stairs, we entered a square whitewashed room: two divans, two windows, one looking on the mountains, the other on the town.

. . . Kuchuk Hanem is a tall, splendid creature, lighter in coloring than an Arab; she comes from Damascus; her skin, particularly on her body, is slightly coffee-coloured. When she bends, her flesh ripples into bronze ridges. Her eyes are dark and enormous. her eyebrows black, her nostrils open and wide; heavy shoulders, full, apple-shaped breasts. She wore a large tarboosh, ornamented on the top with a convex gold disk, in the middle of which was a small green stone imitating emerald; the blue tassel of her tarboosh was spread out fanwise and fell down over her shoulders; just in front of the lower edge of the tarboosh, fastened to her hair and going from one ear to the other, she had a small spray of white artificial flowers. Her black hair, wavy, unruly, pulled straight back on each side from a center parting beginning at the forehead; small braids joined together at the nape of her neck. She has one upper incisor, right, which is beginning to go bad. For a bracelet she has two bands of gold, twisted together and interlaced, around one wrist. Triple necklace of large hollow gold beads. Earrings: gold disks, slightly convex, circumference decorated with gold granules. On her right arm is tattooed a line of blue writing.

She asks us if we would like a little entertainment, but Max says that first he would like to entertain himself alone with her, and they go downstairs. After he finishes, I go down and follow his example. Ground-floor room, with a divan and a *cafas* [an upturned palm-fibre basket] with a mattress.

Dance. The musicians arrive: a child and an old man, whose left eye is covered with a rag; they both scrape on the *rebabah*, a kind of small round violin with a metal leg that rests on the ground and two horse-hair strings. The neck of the instrument is very long in proportion to the rest. Nothing could be more discordant or disagreeable. The musicians never stop playing for an instant unless you shout at them to do so.

Kuchuk Hanem and Bambeh begin to dance. Kuchuk's dance is brutal. She squeezes her bare breasts together with her jacket. She puts on a girdle fashioned from a brown shawl with gold stripes, with three tassels hanging on ribbons. She rises first on one foot, then on the other—marvellous movement: when one foot is on the ground, the other moves up and across in front of the shin-bone—the whole thing with a light bound. I have seen this dance on old Greek vases.

Bambeh prefers a dance on a straight line; she moves with a lowering and raising of one hip only, a kind of rhythmic limping of great character. Bambeh has henna on her hands. She seems to be a devoted servant to Kuchuk. (She was a chambermaid in Cairo in an Italian household and understands a few words of Italian; her eyes are slightly diseased.) All in all, their dancing—except Kuchuk's step mentioned above—is far less good than that of Hasan el-Belbeissi, the male dancer in Cairo. Joseph's opinion is that all beautiful women dance badly.

Kuchuk took up a *darabukeh*. When she plays it, she assumes a superb pose: the *darabukeh* is on her knees, or rather on her left thigh; the left elbow is lowered, the left wrist raised, and the fingers, as they play, fall quite widely apart on the skin of the *darabukeh*; the right hand strikes flatly, marking the rhythm. She leans her head slightly back, in a stiffened pose, the whole body slightly arched.

Ces dames, and particularly the old musician, imbibe considerable amounts of *raki*. Kuchuk dances with my tarboosh on her head. Then she accompanies us to the end of her quarter, climbing up on our backs and making faces and jokes like any Christian tart.

At the café of *ces dames*. We take a cup of coffee. The place is like all such places—flat roof of sugar-cane stalks put together any which way. Kuchuk's amusement at seeing our shaven heads and hearing Max say: '*Allah il allah*,' etc.

Second and more detailed visit to the temple. We wait for the effendi in the café, to give him a letter. Dinner.

We return to Kuchuk's house. The room was lighted by three wicks in glasses full of oil, inserted in tin sconces hanging on the wall. The musicians are in their places. Several glasses of *raki* are quickly drunk; our gift of liquor and the fact that we are wearing swords have their effect.

Arrival of Safiah Zugairah, a small woman with a large nose and eyes that are dark, deep-set, savage, sensual; her necklace of coins clanks like a country cart; she kisses our hands.

The four women seated in a line on the divan singing. The lamps cast quivering, lozenge-shaped shadows on the walls, the light is yellow. Bambeh wore a pink robe with large sleeves (all the costumes are light-colored) and her hair was covered with a black kerchief such as the fellahin wear. They all sang, the *darabukehs* throbbed, and the monotonous rebecs furnished a soft but shrill bass; it was like a rather gay song of mourning.

Coup with Safia Zugairah ('Little Sophie')—I stain the divan. She is very corrupt and writhing, extremely voluptuous. But the best was the second copulation with Kuchuk. Effect of her necklace between my teeth. Her cunt felt like rolls of velvet as she made me come. I felt like a tiger.

Kuchuk dances the Bee. First, so that the door can be closed, the women send away Farghali and another sailor, who up to now have been watching the dances and who, in the background, constituted the grotesque element of the scene. A black veil is tied around the eyes of the child, and a fold of his blue turban is lowered over those of the old man. Kuchuk shed her clothing as she danced. Finally she was naked except for a *fichu* which she held in her hands and behind which she pretended to hide, and at the end she threw down the *fichu*. That was the Bee. She danced it very briefly and said she does not like to dance that dance. Joseph, very excited, kept clapping his hands: '*La, eu, nia, oh! eu, nia, oh!*' Finally, after repeating for us the wonderful step she had danced in the afternoon, she sank down breathless on her divan, her body continuing to move slightly in rhythm. One of the women threw her her enormous white trousers striped with pink, and she pulled them on up to her neck. The two musicians were unblindfolded.

When she was sitting cross-legged on the divan, the magnificent, absolutely sculptural design of her knees.

Another dance: a cup of coffee is placed on the ground; she dances before it, then falls on her knees and continues to move her torso, always clacking the castanets, and describing in the air a gesture with her arms as though she were swimming. That continues, gradually the head is lowered, she reaches the cup, takes the edge of it between her teeth, and then leaps up quickly with a single bound.

She was not too enthusiastic about having us spend the night with her, out of fear of thieves who are apt to come when they know strangers are there. Some guards or pimps (on whom she did not spare the cudgel) slept downstairs in a side room, with Joseph and the negress, an Abyssinian slave who carried on each arm the round scar (like a burn) of a plague-sore. We went to bed; she insisted on keeping the outside. Lamp: the wick rested in an oval cup with a lip; after some violent play, *coup*. She falls asleep with her hand in mine. She snores. The lamp, shining feebly, cast a triangular gleam, the color of pale metal, on her beautiful forehead; the rest of her face was in shadow. Her little dog slept on my silk jacket on the divan. Since she complained of a cough, I put my pelisse over her blanket. I heard Joseph and the guards talking in low voices; I gave myself over to intense reverie, full of reminiscences. Feeling of her stomach against my buttocks. Her mound warmer than her stomach, heated me like a hot iron. Another time I dozed off with my fingers passed through her necklace, as though to hold her should she awake. I thought of Judith and Holofernes sleeping together. At quarter of three, we awake—another *coup*, this time very affectionate. We told each other a great many things by pressure. (As she slept she kept contracting her hands and thighs mechanically, like involuntary shudders.)

I smoke a *sheesheh*, she goes down to talk with Joseph, brings back a bucket of burning charcoal, warms herself, comes back to bed. '*Basta !*'

How flattering it would be to one's pride if at the moment of leaving you were sure that you left a memory behind, that she would think of you more than of the others who have been there, that you would remain in her heart!

In the morning we said goodbye very calmly.*

Our two sailors come to carry our things to the *cange*, and after returning to it I do some shooting around Esna. A cotton field under palms and *gassis*. Arabs, donkeys and buffalo going to the fields. The wind was blowing through the slender branches of the *gassis*, whistling as it does in the reeds at home. The sun climbs, the hills are no longer pale pink as they were this morning as I left Kuchuk Hanem's house; the fresh air feels good on my eyes ... I thought a great deal about that morning (Michaelmas) at the Marquis de Pomereu's, at l'Héron, when I walked all

* The notebooks contain a few other details about the night with Kuchuk Hanem that are not included in the rewritten notes, among them a simple expletive, 'Oh Zeïnab', apparently favored by Kuchuk, invoking the daughter of the Prophet, and an observation of insect life that was later to arouse comment (see p. 220):

'To shield herself from the lighted charcoal, she put the blanket over her head.

'"*Ia Zeïnab, ia Zeïnab*," with the first syllable accented.

'My face turned toward the wall, and without changing my position, I amused myself killing bedbugs on the wall.'

by myself in the park, after the ball: it was during the holidays between my forth and third forms.*

I return to the boat and get Joseph . . . We buy meat, a belt.

. . . We meet Bambeh and the fourth woman who played the *darabukeh*; Bambeh saw to our supply of bread; she looked extremely tired.

We left Esna at a quarter before noon.† Some Bedouins sold us a gazelle they had killed that morning on the other side of the Nile.

Temple of Esna. . . . This temple is 33 m. 70 long and 16 m. 89 wide, the circumference of the columns is 5 m. 37, the total height of the columns is 11 m. 37. There are 24 columns . . . An Arab climbed on to the capital of a column to drop the metric tape. A yellow cow, on the left, poked her head inside . . .

Saturday, 9 March 1850. Assuan. Reached Assuan threading our course between the rocks in midstream; they are dark chocolate-color, with long white streaks of bird-droppings that widen toward the bottom. To the right, bare sand-hills, their summits sharp against the blue sky. The light comes down perpendicular into transparent depths. A negro landscape.

* How consciously did Flaubert remember this particular page of his notebook when he wrote on one and the same page in *Madame Bovary* two sentences that begin: 'The whistling wind would flatten the reeds and rustle the trembling beech leaves . . .' and: 'Then, late in September, something exceptional happened: she was invited to La Vaubyessard, home of the Marquis d'Andervilliers?'

† Du Camp, in his account of the visit to Kuchuk Hanem published in *Le Nil*, makes no mention of having 'entertained himself' privately with her, and says that immediately following the end of the dancing 'I said good-bye to Kuchuk Hanem and regained my *cange*, which left with a good wind about four in the morning.'

. . . The Governor, on his doorstep, raises both hands to his turban in salute to our *firmans*; beside him, a big fat blond personage wearing several coats—the former governor of Wadi Halfa. A man is brought to him who found some money on the island of Elephantine; he declared it, but he is given the third degree nevertheless, to make sure that he hasn't kept a few coins for himself. Also an army deserter, and a splendidly shaped little Nubian girl whose height they measure with a stick in order to assess the tax that every slave-trader has to pay per head.

In a shop we see an *almeh*, tall, slender, black—or rather, green—frizzy negro hair. Her eyes are dreamy and sad, or, rather, suggestive of negro daydreaming. She rolls her eyes—she is charming in profile. Another, little woman with tousled frizzy hair under her tarboosh—this one is cheerful.

Azizeh. The tall girl is named Azizeh. Her dancing is more expert than Kuchuk's. For dancing she takes off her flowing robe and puts on a cotton dress of European cut. She begins. Her neck slides back and forth on her vertebrae, and more often sideways, as though her head were going to fall off; terrifying effect of decapitation.

She stands on one foot, lifts the other, the knee making a right angle, then brings it down firmly. This is no longer Egypt; it is negro, African, savage—as wild as the other was formal.

Another dance: putting the left foot in the place of the right, and the right in the place of the left, alternately and very fast.

The blanket that served as rug in her hut became wrinkled; she stopped from time to time to pull it straight.

She stripped. On her belly she wore a belt of colored beads. Her long necklace of gold piastres descended to her vagina, and she passed the end of it through the bead belt.

Furious jerking of the hips. The face always expressionless. A little girl of two or three, affected by the music, tried to imitate her, and danced herself, making no sound.

This was in an earthen hut, scarcely high enough for a woman to stand erect, in a section outside the city that was almost completely reduced to ruins. In the midst of this silence, these women in red and gold.

On the shore, a man holding ostrich plumes offers them to us for sale.

In 1850 there were no dams or locks on the Nile, and boats on their way to Wadi Halfa were lightened of their ballast and cargo and conveyed through the First Cataract (just beyond Assuan) in the manner Flaubert describes.

FROM FLAUBERT'S TRAVEL NOTES

Monday, 11 March. In the morning we make ready to pass the Cataract and set out with two special *raïs* and a Nubian pilot (Raïs Hasan) who is to take us to Wadi Halfa.

Our pilot—old, wrinkled, with a great nose, hunched over the tiller, looking far ahead. Children astride palm logs jump into the foaming whirlpools and disappear; you can see the front of their log rear up as they surface; they climb on to the deck streaming with water. They are like bronze statues on fountains, dripping and gleaming in the sun. Nubians' teeth are longer, wider, and spaced further apart than those of Arabs, and their muscular system is less sturdy.

... At half past noon we stop below the Cataract and spend the night in a little cove among the rocks ...

Tuesday, 12 [March 1850. Assuan]. We set out at seven in the morning. The big sail of our *cange* passes between the rocks, at times touching them. Seen from the shore when it is at rest with its two sails unfurled, it looks like a great bird (a crane), its wings outspread but its head hidden under its legs.

One of the men jumps into the water to bring the cable from the other bank. I walk barefoot on the rocks, guided by the son of a sheik of a neighbouring village who came to work on board the day before. A cable is fastened on one side so that the boat does not swerve, and it is pulled ahead with a second cable.

An old *raïs* (Dushi) climbs on to the rocks simply to shout; perched there like a monkey and waving his arms, he produced a repertory of shrill cries, apparently much more concerned that the men should follow his rhythm than with how they were hauling on the cable. Sometimes the entire front half of the boat would be under water, while the stern, already lifted from the lower level, hung in the air. A long row of men on the rocks, hauling in unison and singing. The *cange* covered with men pushing, shouting, singing; noise of the water, of children jumping in, streaming bodies emerging, foam around black rocks, sun, yellow sand.

While the cange *was being passed through the First Cataract, Max stayed on board, but Flaubert and Joseph were guided along the shore to the Cataract's end.*

We walk through the center of a small Nubian village. A soldier (in green) wants to arrest my guide because of some quarrel the day before; I arrange matters. Little girl naked except for a leather fringe and necklace and bracelets of colored beads; her hair is curled and cut short over the forehead so as to form a horse-shoe shape.

. . . I get into the dinghy and am rowed by two small boys to the village of Mahatta, where the *cange* is to arrive. Clusters of palms enclosed by low circular walls, against which Turks sit smoking; it was like an engraving, an oriental scene in a book.

A rachitic child was dragging himself in the dust; his thighs were no thicker than the lower part of his legs, and his back was humped as though his spine were broken. In the Nubian village I walked through with Joseph, he showed me a child's toy consisting of a small piece of wood to which were attached a few leather thongs, some of them trimmed with colored beads, the whole thing wrapped in three or four rags gray with dust.

We re-embark our luggage, which has been transported overland by camel. Sassetti laden with arms.

FLAUBERT TO LOUIS BOUILHET

13 March 1850
On board our cange, *12 leagues beyond Assuan.*
. . . In six or seven hours we are going to pass the Tropic of that well-known personage Cancer. It is 30 degrees * in the shade at this moment, we are barefoot and clad in nothing but shirts, and I am writing to you on my divan, to the sound of the *darabukehs* of our sailors, who are singing and clapping their hands.

* Réaumur. 86° Fahrenheit.

The sun is beating down mercilessly on the awning over our deck. The Nile is as flat as a river of steel. On its banks are clusters of tall palms. The sky is blue as blue. *O pauvre vieux ! pauvre vieux de mon cœur !*

What are you doing, you in Rouen? It is a long time since I had any of your letters, or rather I have so far had only one, dated the end of December, and which I answered immediately. Perhaps another has arrived in Cairo and is being sent on to me. My mother writes that she sees you very seldom. Why is that? If it bores you too much, go once in a while anyway, for my sake, and try to tell me everything you can about what is going on in my house in every possible respect. Have you been in Paris again and seen Gautier and Pradier?* What has happened to the trip to England for your Chinese story? *Melaenis* must be finished? Send me the end, you bloody bastard. I often growl out some of your lines, if you want to know. I must without further delay withdraw as vociferously as possible the objection I made to your word *vagabond* as applied to the Nile:

'*Que le Nil vagabond roule sur ses rivages.*'

There is no designation more just, more precise and at the same time more all-embracing. It is a crazy, magnificent river, more like an ocean than anything else. Sandy beaches extend as far as the eye can see on both its banks, blown about by the wind like sea beaches; it is so enormous that one doesn't know where the current is, and sometimes you feel enclosed in a great lake. Ah! But if you expect a proper letter

* The sculptor James Pradier, who had introduced Flaubert to Louise Colet and whose wife, from whom he was separated, was to be (along with Louise Colet and several other women and Flaubert himself) a model for Emma Bovary.

you are mistaken. I warn you seriously that my intelligence has greatly diminished. This worries me: *I am not joking*—I feel very empty, very flat, very sterile. What am I to do once back in the old lodgings? Publish or not publish? The *Saint Anthony* business** dealt me a heavy blow, I don't mind telling you. I have tried in vain to do something with my oriental tale, and for a day or two I played with the story of Mykerinos in Herodotus (the king who slept with his daughter). But it all came to nothing. By way of work, every day I read the *Odyssey* in Greek. Since we have been on the Nile I have done four books; we are coming home by way of Greece, so it may be of use to me. The first days on board I began to write a little; but I was not long, thank God, in realizing the ineptitude of such behavior; just now it is best for me to be all eyes. We live, therefore, in the grossest idleness, stretched out all day on our divans watching everything that goes by: camels, herds of oxen from the Sennaar, boats floating down to Cairo laden with negresses and elephants' tusks. We are now, my dear sir, in a land where women go naked—one might say with the poet 'naked as the hand,' for by way of costume they wear only rings. I have lain with Nubian girls whose necklaces of gold piastres hung down to their thighs and whose black stomachs were encircled by colored beads—they feel cold when you rub your own stomach against them. And their dancing! *Sacré nom de Dieu!!!* But let us proceed in proper order.

From Cairo to Benisuef, nothing very interesting.

... At a place called Gebel el-Teir we had an amusing sight. On the top of a hill overlooking the Nile there is a Coptic monastery, whose monks have

* Its condemnation by Bouilhet and Du Camp, see Chap. I.

the habit, as soon as they see a boatload of tourists, of running down, throwing themselves in the water, and swimming out to ask for alms. Everyone who passes is assailed by them. You see these fellows, totally naked, rushing down their perpendicular cliffs and swimming towards you as fast as they can, shouting: '*Baksheesh, baksheesh, cawadja christiani!*' And since there are many caves in the cliff at this particular spot, echo repeats '*Cawadja, cawadja!*' loud as a cannon. Vultures and eagles were flying overhead, the boat was darting through the water, its two great sails very full. At that moment one of our sailors, the clown of the crew, began to dance a naked, lascivious dance that consisted of an attempt to bugger himself. To drive off the Christians he showed them his prick and his arse pretending to piss and shit on their heads (they were clinging to the sides of the *cange*). The other sailors shouted insults at them, repeating the names of Allah and Mohammed. Some hit them with sticks, others with ropes; Joseph rapped their knuckles with his kitchen tongs. It was a *tutti* of cudgelings, pricks, bare arses, yells and laughter. As soon as they were given money they put it in their mouths and returned home via the route they had come. If they weren't greeted with a good beating, the boats would be assailed by such hordes of them that there would be danger of capsizing.

In another place it's not men who call on you, but birds. At Sheik Sa'id there is a tomb chapel built in honor of a Moslem saint where birds go of their own accord and drop food that is given to them—this food is then offered to poor travelers—(You and I, *who have read Voltaire*, don't believe this. But everyone is so backward here! You so seldom hear anyone singing the songs of Béranger! 'What, sir, the benefits of civilization are not being introduced into this country? Where are your railway networks? What is the state of elementary education? Etc.')—so that as you sail past this chapel all the birds flock around the boat and land on the rigging—you throw them bits of bread, they wheel about, pick it up from the water, and fly off.

At Kena I did something suitable, which I trust will win your approval: we had landed to buy supplies and were walking peacefully and dreamily in the bazaars, inhaling the odor of sandalwood that floated about us, when suddenly, at a turn in the street, we found ourselves in the whores' quarter. Picture to yourself, my friend, five or six curving streets lined with hovels about four feet high, built of dried gray mud. In the doorways, women standing or sitting on straw mats. The negresses had dresses of sky-blue; others were in yellow, in white, in red—loose garments fluttering in the hot wind. Odors of spices. On their bare breasts long necklaces of gold piastres, so that when they move they rattle like carts. They call after you in drawling voices: '*Cawadja, cawadja*,' their white teeth gleaming between their red or black lips, their metallic eyes rolling like wheels. I walked through those streets and walked through them again, giving *baksheesh* to all the women, letting them call me and catch hold of me; they took me around the waist and tried to pull me into their houses—think of all that, with the sun blazing down on it. Well, I abstained. (Young Du Camp did not follow my example.)* I abstained deliberately, in order to pre-

* In his account of the prostitutes' quarter at Kena published in *Le Nil*, Du Camp says: 'It makes one understand the great Biblical images, and I went away repeating the verse of Jeremiah: "I have seen thine adulteries, and thy neighings, the

serve the sweet sadness of the scene and engrave it deeply in my memory. In this way I went away dazzled, and have remained so. There is nothing more beautiful than these women calling you. If I had gone with any of them, a second picture would have been superimposed on the first and dimmed its splendor.

I haven't always made such sacrifices on the altar of art. At Esna in one day I came five times and sucked three. I say it straight out and without circumlocution, and let me add that I enjoyed it. Kuchuk Hanem is a famous courtesan. When we reached her house she was waiting for us; her confidante had come that morning to the *cange* escorted by a tame sheep all spotted with yellow henna and with a black velvet muzzle on its nose, that followed her like a dog—it was quite a sight. She had just left her bath. She was wearing a large tarboosh.*

. . . That night we returned to Kuchuk Hanem's: there were four women dancers and singers—*almehs*. (The word *almeh* means 'learned woman,' 'bluestocking,' or 'whore'—which proves, Monsieur, that in all countries women of letters . . .!!!)† . . . When it was time to leave I didn't leave . . . I sucked her furiously—her body was covered with sweat—she was tired after dancing—she was cold—I covered her with my pelisse, and she fell asleep with her fingers in

---

lewdness of thy whoredom, and thine abominations on the hills and in the fields."' The last words of Du Camp's translation read: '*Je connais tes fornications*,' which one supposes he did not mean his readers to apply to him personally.

* I have omitted several passages concerning Kuchuk Hanem transcribed into this letter almost exactly from the travel notes.

† An allusion to Louise Colet.

mine. As for me, I scarcely shut my eyes. Watching that beautiful creature asleep (she snored, her head against my arm: I had slipped my forefinger under her necklace), my night was one long, infinitely intense reverie—that was why I stayed. I thought of my nights in Paris brothels—a whole series of old memories came back—and I thought of her, of her dance, of her voice as she sang songs that for me were without meaning and even without distinguishable words. That continued all night. At three o'clock I got up to piss in the street—the stars were shining. The sky was clear and immensely distant. She awoke, went to get a pot of charcoal and for an hour crouched beside it warming herself, then she came back to bed and fell asleep again. As for the *coups*, they were good—the third especially was ferocious, and the last tender—we told each other many sweet things—toward the end there was something sad and loving in the way we embraced.

... In my absorption in all those things, *mon pauvre vieux*, you never ceased to be present. The thought of you was like a constant vesicant, inflaming my mind and making its juices flow by adding to the stimulation. I was sorry (the word is weak) that you were not there—I enjoyed it all for myself and for you—the excitement was for both of us, and you came in for a good share, you may be sure.

... Just now we have stopped for lack of wind—the flies are stinging my face. Young Du Camp has gone off to take a picture. He is doing quite well; I think we'll have a nice album. As regards vice, he is calming down; it seems to us that I am inheriting his qualities, for I am growing lewd. Such is my profound conviction. When the brain sinks the prick rises. That isn't to say that I haven't collected a few metaphors. I have had a few stirrings. But how to make use of them, and when?

... [*p. s.*] Max insists that for the sake of elegance I add ... '23° 39′ North Latitude.' We are now exactly under the Tropic ...

Thursday, 19 [*March 1850*]. [*Above Derr.*] Did about seven leagues. In the afternoon we board two boats belonging to slave traders, on their way down-river to Cairo. Bought belts and amulets.

The gellabs' boats. The master of the first was a large man with black side-whiskers; we climb up on to the roof of the cabin and he presents us with bunches of ostrich plumes. The masts have been taken down, the boat is proceeding by oar, the black women are all packed in, in all kinds of positions. Some are grinding flour between stones, their hair hanging down in front of them like the long mane of a horse when it eats from the ground. With the movement of grinding, their breasts sway, as do their braids and the ends of the leather thongs binding them. A mother with her small child. One woman was arranging another's hair. A little girl from the Gondar plateau with piastres on her forehead; she stood motionless and placid while Maxime fastened the necklace of mercury beads around her neck. All these faces are calm, nothing irritated in their expression—brutes take these things as a matter of course. As we were leaving, the *gellab*, in order to get a few more necklaces out of us, brought from the cabin two or three of the best women, or those closest to the door.

(131)

One Abyssinian, tall, haughty, hand on hip as she watches us go.

Second boat: the trader wears a white turban. We sit under the awning, on a webbed divan. One woman is having her hair combed with a porcupine quill: the thin braids are undone one by one and then rebraided.

The *gellabs* offer us, for sale, fine bags and some gourds; the one on the second boat, a kind of leather water jar with two handles, which can be carried by a strap.

These women are gashed with tattooing; in the second boat there was one whose back was marked in this way from top to bottom; there were rows of welts or ridges all across her lower back, the scars of cuts made with a hot iron. On all these boats, among the women, there are old negresses who make and re-make the trip continually; they are there to console the new slaves and keep up their spirits; they teach them to resign themselves to their fate and they act as interpreters between them and the trader, an Arab.

In certain sunsets, the clouds stream down from a great crest—like the strands of a luminous mane (a horse's mane). Clouds mottle the surface of the Nile with great plaques of pale blue.

Friday, 22 [March 1850]. We touch the beach at Wadi Halfa as we are finishing dinner. Moonlight so bright on the sand that it looks like snow. An eighth of a league away (to the left), a row of palms with a few houses: that is the entire village. To the right, on the other side of the Nile, is the desert, with two conical hills (their peaks sliced off), very broad at the base.

On the beach, an Arab engineer who speaks excellent French; also Khalil Effendi and another effendi,* a Nubian in a white shirt that fluttered in the moonlight. (The wind had been strong all day and carried us along well.) Visit with these three gentlemen . . .

Saturday, 23 [March 1850]. Excursion to Gebel Abusir,† via the desert of Abu Salim, left bank of the Nile.

Sunday, 24 March. Palm Sunday. [Second excursion to Gebel Abusir.] Left at six in the morning in our dinghy for the Cataract, with Raïs Hasan and three other Nubians from the First Cataract. I had with me a little raïs of about fourteen, Mohammed; he is yellow-skinned, a silver earring in his left ear. He rowed strongly and gracefully, shouted, and as we rode the currents he led everybody singing; his arms were charmingly modeled, with firm young biceps. He had slipped his left arm out of its sleeve, so that on his entire right side he was as though draped, with his left side and part of his belly uncovered. Slender waist. Folds on his belly that rose and fell as he leaned forward on his oar. His voice was vibrant as he sang: 'El naby, el naby' ['The Prophet, the Prophet']. He was a child of the water, of the tropical sun, of the free life, full of distinction and nobility. And full of childish courtesy—gave me dates and lifted the end of my blanket that was trailing in the water.

---

* Du Camp, in Le Nil, identifies these two effendis as the Sheik of Wadi Halfa and the Nazir of Ibrim, who was on a tax-collecting tour and whom we shall meet again. Apparently this Khalil Effendi (if Flaubert got his name right) was not their teacher from Cairo.

† One of the two 'conical hills' mentioned in the preceding entry, a favorite tourist spot for viewing the Second Cataract and a stretch of Lower Nubia.

Several vultures were perched on the rocks; and washed up at the foot of one rock was an old crocodile. That evening we saw the same vultures again, and nearby a jackal, which ran off as we approached.

I reach the foot of Gebel Abusir at nine, and fire a few rifle shots to call Maxime. From the distance a black rock, shining in the sun, gives the effect of a Nubian in a white shirt on look-out, or of a white cloth hung out to dry. How can something black come to look white in this way? It happens when the sun strikes the edge of an angle. I have frequently observed the same effect, and Gibert tells me that he too has noticed it, in Rome.*

I lunch under the tent, in full sun. I had stretched out on the ground in search of a little shade, but the shade wasn't long in disappearing.

Walk around the two adjacent rocky hills. The tent was in front of them, before the Cataract (that is to say, *beside* the Cataract). As we rounded the first hill, we came to a great rolling stretch of sand on the desert side. From here (with one's back to the desert, of course) one sees the Cataract in the distance. From the top of the second hill you see the desert—first rolling, then stretching away in great flat lines. I return to the tent alone, via the desert and behind the hills. Silence. Silence. Silence. The sunlight beats down—it is of a black transparency. I walk over small stones, my head bent, the sun searing my skull.

Return to Wadi Halfa in the dinghy, with Maxime. Little Mohammed is as he was this morning. We are rocked by the wind and the waves; night falls; the waves slap the bow of our dinghy, and it pitches, the moon rises. In the position in which I was sitting, it

* Did Flaubert's observation of 'black coming to look white' owe something to Du Camp's negatives?

was shining on my right leg and the portion of my white sock that was between my trouser and my shoe.

[Flaubert's] future novel engrossed him. 'I am obsessed by it,' he would say to me. Amid African landscapes he dreamed of Norman landscapes. On the borders of Lower Nubia, on the summit of Gebel Abusir, which overlooks the Second Cataract, as we were watching the Nile dash itself against the sharp black granite rocks, he gave a cry: 'I have found it! Eureka! Eureka! I will call her Emma Bovary!' And he repeated it several times; he savored the name Bovary, pronouncing the 'o' very short.

Of all Du Camp's reportages about Flaubert, that one has aroused the greatest disbelief among Flaubertistes, both because Flaubert himself makes no mention of the episode and especially because it was not until after Flaubert's return to France that Louis Bouilhet told him of the death of the medical officer Eugene Delamare and urged him to 'write up' the story of him and his wife—the story that was to become Madame Bovary. *However, the skeptics may just possibly be doing Du Camp an injustice here, as well as displaying a certain literary naïveté in linking* Madame Bovary *too closely, or too exclusively, to the real-life story of the Delamares. As we have seen, two years before leaving for Egypt, Flaubert had made a note in Blois about a possible story of provincial life: 'some deep, great, intimate story being lived here amid these peaceful dwellings, a passion like a sickness, lasting until death . . .' Sensational and Du Camp-like as the shouting of 'Eureka!*

*. . . Emma Bovary!' from the top of the rock Abusir
may seem, Jean Bruneau has suggested that it may well
have taken place, with 'Emma Bovary'—her name
adapted from that of the hotel-keeper in Cairo—being in
Flaubert's mind at that time not Emma Bovary as we
know her, but the heroine of the story imagined in Blois
or of, simply, whatever provincial novel he might write.
That the possibility of a provincial novel continued in
his mind throughout the 'Oriental' journey is certain,**
and Du Camp's testimony may be quite the opposite of
false—it may be an additional confirmation.*

*Less often noticed, but at least as eloquent of the
proximity of* Madame Bovary *in Flaubert's life as the
'Eureka!' on Gebel Abusir reported by Du Camp, is a
passage in the travel notes written the day of the second
visit to that very rock, a passage quoted just above and
worth repeating here:*

> *Return to Wadi Halfa in the dinghy, with Maxime.
> Little Mohammed is as he was this morning. Rocked by
> the wind and the waves; night falls; the waves slap the
> bow of our dinghy, and it pitches; the moon rises. In the
> position in which I am sitting, it was shining on my right
> leg and the portion of my white sock that was between
> my trouser and my shoe.*

*A minor paragraph, perhaps, in the chronicle of a long
Nile journey; but one of the purest and most concentrated
pieces of mature Flaubertian writing that we have before
the great novels. All-enveloping nature; then, closer, the
effect of nature on the immediate scene; and finally,
closest of all, a single, homely foreground detail—a leg
with part of a white sock in the moonlight. One can easily
see how contemporary readers of many similar passages
in* Madame Bovary, *accustomed as they were to moon-
drenched Romantic landscapes, might feel that the*

* See Epilogue, p. 216.

(136)

Realist Flaubert was wasting his moonlight on a mere white sock, and at the same time how they would be uneasily, reluctantly aware of the poetry of the whole. And pervading that return in the dinghy is the presence of the charming young Mohammed, with his yellow skin and silver earring, much as the fascination of Emma Bovary, an exotic in her provincial town, will pervade the Norman scenes of the novel.

FROM FLAUBERT TO HIS MOTHER

24 March [1850]. Palm Sunday.
... This will come to you from Wadi Halfa—in other words, from the outermost point of our journey. Making more or less lengthy detours, we'll now be doing nothing but coming gradually closer to you ...

FROM FLAUBERT'S TRAVEL NOTES

Monday, [25 March 1850]. At nine in the morning I set out alone for the Cataract on donkey-back, planning to kill the jackal we saw last night near the dead crocodile. My donkey is uncontrollable—will go only sideways. I return on foot after half an hour, via the riverbank; I had set out from behind Wadi Halfa. This morning, on his way to photograph the Cataract, Max saw in the distance a camel running, with something dark and short behind it: it was a runaway slave of the *gellabs*, who was being brought back like this, tied to the camel.

We leave Wadi Halfa at noon. The masts of the *cange* have been taken down.

VII

Down the
Nile to Thebes

*Now there began what was for Du Camp the heart of the
Egyptian journey: the descent of the Nile, with stops
wherever there were monuments to be photographed and
inscriptions to be reproduced by 'squeezes.'*

FROM 'LE NIL, EGYPTE ET NUBIE'
BY MAXIME DU CAMP

[*Wadi Halfa, 25 March 1850*]. My *cange* is now set
for the descent of the river. The two masts and the
yards have been taken down, strong thole-pins have
been inserted in the gunwales, the oars are in place,
and we are ready to leave.

Twelve sailors are on their feet, six on each side of
the boat, each of them grasping an oar eighteen feet
long; the mate has taken the rudder; Raïs Ibrahim
has given the signal, we cast off the line that tied us to
the bank, and we move off with the current. The
sailors strike up a monotonous chant that accompanies
and eases their work; the muffled sound of twelve
oars rhythmically striking the water articulates each
verset of their song. For three and a half months I was
to see them—all day and sometimes at night as well—
wielding their oars, straining against headwinds, worn

with fatigue, sleeping few hours at best, but always courageous and always chanting their melancholy refrain, whose sweet, slow notes still hum in my memory. During this late season of the year the Nile is at its lowest, so every day, and often several times a day, my boat would go aground on the sand; then the men would drop their oars, doff their clothes, jump into the water, and with great exertion lift the keel stuck in the bed of the river. We would hear stifled cries that were like moans, then the cries would come faster and faster, quick and gay like the sounds of a party; and the boat would resume its way as the sailors jumped aboard, climbing over the sides, their shoulders often bloody. *Allah Akbar!* God is the greatest! And back to the oars.

It was during this part of the trip that Du Camp, determined photographer, took the largest number of the pictures, chiefly of temples, that were to compose his published volume. The collection has become famous as the first photographic record of many of the Egyptian monuments before they were systematically cleared of sand later in the century—and simply as a group of 'primitive' (and excellent) photographs. His pictures won the Cross of the Légion d'Honneur for Du Camp, who in making them perhaps felt that he was carrying on a family tradition: his mother's brother had married the daughter of Champollion, the decipherer of the Rosetta Stone.*

In Le Nil *Du Camp included several dozen pages of descriptions of the temples he photographed. In later life he remembered Flaubert's participation in this part of the journey as follows:*

* See Bibliographical Note, p. 230.

Gustave Flaubert shared none of my exultation; he
was quiet and withdrawn. He was averse to movement
and action. He would have liked to travel, if he could,
stretched out on a sofa and not stirring, watching landscapes, ruins and cities pass before him like the screen
of a panorama* mechanically unwinding. From our
very first days in Cairo I had been aware of his lassitude and boredom: this journey, which he had so
cherished as a dream and whose realization had
seemed to him impossible, did not satisfy him. I was
very direct; I said to him: 'If you wish to return to
France I will give you my servant to go with you.'
He replied: 'No, I began it, and I'll go through with
it; you take care of the itineraries and I'll fit in—it's
the same to me whether I go right or left.' The temples
seemed to him always alike, the mosques and the landscapes all the same. I am not sure that when gazing
on the island of Elephantine he did not sigh for the
meadows of Sotteville, or long for the Seine when he
saw the Nile. At Philae he settled himself comfortably
in the cool shade of one of the halls of the great temple
of Isis to read *Gerfaut*, by Charles de Bernard, which
he had bought in Cairo.

The thought of his mother continually drew him in
the direction of Croisset, and he had not got over the
setback he had experienced with *Saint Anthony*.

* Panoramas—the mechanical kind, the pre-photographic
moving pictures—were on Du Camp's mind while writing
about Egypt, for on the Nile he and Flaubert encountered
Colonel Jean-Charles Langlois, celebrated at the time as painter
of several of the great historical panoramas that delighted Paris
audiences: 'The Battle of the Pyramids,' 'The Burning of
Moscow,' etc. The Colonel had been making preparatory
drawings for 'The Ruins of Karnak.'

Often of an evening, when the water murmured softly around our boat and the Southern Cross shone out among the stars, we would talk over this book which was so close to his heart.*

In 1850 the rock temples and colossal statues at Abu Simbel were all but buried in sand: it was only later in the century, after the coming of the British to Egypt, that they and most of the other antique monuments were properly cleared. In the 1960s the colossi were chopped free from the rock, hoisted in sections to the top of the cliff, and re-assembled; and today the waters of Lake Nasser, created by the construction of the Assuan High Dam and flooding much of Upper Nubia, cover the site where Du Camp superintended 'clearing operations to disengage the chin of one of the exterior colossi' for his photography while Flaubert dreamed of Norman farms. Others of the Upper-Nubian temples, too, have been dismantled for reconstruction elsewhere.

FROM FLAUBERT'S TRAVEL NOTES

[*27 March 1850*]. *Abu Simbel*. The colossi. Effect of the sun seen through the door of the large temple half blocked by sand: as though through an air-hole.

At the far end, three colossi half visible in the shadow. Lying on the ground and blinking, I had the impression that the first colossus on the right was moving its eyelids. Handsome heads, ugly feet.

---

* Flaubert wrote to Louis Bouilhet later, from Damascus: 'I have recovered (not without difficulty) from the frightful blow caused me by *Saint Anthony*. I can't boast that I don't brood about it sometimes still, but I'm no longer sick about it, as I was during the first four months of my trip. I saw everything through the veil that that disappointment had cast over me, and kept repeating to myself the inept words: "What's the use?"'

The bats utter their sharp little cry. For a moment some other animal made a regular sound: it was like a country clock striking in the distance. I thought of Norman farms in summer, when everyone is in the fields, towards three in the afternoon ... and of King Mykerinos riding in his chariot one evening around Lake Moeris with a priest beside him; he tells him of his love for his daughter. This is a harvest evening ... the buffalo are coming home.

... Attempts to make squeezes!!

Small temple: on the pillars, faces looking like wigs stuck on wooden stands.

In the large temple, what is the meaning of a slab of masonry, covered with inscriptions in demotic, between the third and fourth colossi to the left as you enter?

In the large temple, left aisle, fine reliefs of chariots: the ornaments on the horses' heads are complicated, and the horses generally long and saddle-backed.

Holy Thursday. We begin clearing operations, to disengage the chin of one of the exterior colossi.

Good Friday. Clearing: "aou-afi, aou-afi."* Arched body of a frizzy-haired little negro, ugly, his eyes sore from the dust, who was carrying a jar of milk on his head.

In the small temple, many wasps' nests, especially in the corners.

Reflection: the Egyptian temples bore me profoundly. Are they going to become like the churches in Brittany, the waterfalls in the Pyrenees? Oh necessity! To do what you are supposed to do; to be always, according to the circumstances (and despite

* Colloquial greeting among fellahin.

(142)

the aversion of the moment), what a young man, or a tourist, or an artist, or a son, or a citizen, etc. is supposed to be!

31 March [1850]. Easter Sunday. In the afternoon, reach ancient Ibrim, on the right bank of the Nile. While Max took a picture of the fort from below, I slowly climbed the side of the hill, breaking my toenails on rough stones that had rolled down from above. The soil is like cinders. Three or four Arabs passed me on the right, riding donkeys. I walk around the citadel, looking for a way in; finally I find one on the plateau, facing east.

The interior is an entire city enclosed within walls; houses all in ruins and crammed close together or even touching; streets wind between; in the center, a large square. If you climb on to a wall, the foundations of all those ruined houses—the mere four walls—give a checkerboard effect. Ruins of a mosque, with a granite column bearing a Greek cross; similar columns have been made to serve as door-sills in several places. The entrance gate was on the north side. Through openings in the wall one can see long stretches of the Nile—there are broad islands of sand. On the other side of the Nile, the desert; in the desert middle-ground, a single tree on the right; further off, two on the left.

The whole ruin gives off an effluvium of fever, and makes you think of bored people dying of marasmus; it is the Orient of the Middle Ages, the Mamelukes, the Barbarians. The citadel, built on the crest of the rock, formerly belonged to the Mamelukes, who thus controlled the river. Most of it is built of rough stones —in a very few places, chiefly at the corners, the stones are shaped and fitted.

There is a great silence here—not a soul—I am alone, two birds of prey glide overhead; from the other side of the Nile, in the desert, I hear a man's voice calling someone.

I returned [to the *cange*] as night was slowly falling, and watched the darkness engulf everything. To my left, a long ravine leading to the desert; along the side of the ravine winds a path—a hyena track. There are many around here; in the evening the *raïs* warns us not to wander too far from the boat; last year a Turk and his horse were eaten near the First Cataract. Maxime, worried because I was away so long, had sent some of the sailors to find me.

Monday, 1 April. Second visit to the fort, with Maxime. The caves of Ibrim, on the riverbank, eight or nine feet above the waterline, are a good joke: they contain absolutely nothing, a discovery that kept me cheerful the entire rest of the day.

We spend the afternoon stretched out on the bow of the boat, on Raïs Ibrahim's mat, talking—and not without a certain sadness and bitterness—about that old topic: literature—sweet and never-ending obsession!

Tuesday, 2 April. Korosko. Khamsin weather—heavy, the sun hidden by clouds. On our arrival here at noon, the heat was like blasts from an oven (literally); one feels one's very lungs (I mean it) seared by the gusts of hot wind . . .

Beginning now, at the temple of Es-Sebuʿa, and at succeeding temples, Flaubert jotted down a few details in his notebook, and usually expanded them a little in the rewritten version. They are remarkably devoid of personal touches, sound dutiful rather than interested, and have for the most part been omitted here.

[*3 April*]. *Es-Sebu'a* ... the temple itself is completely buried in the sand ... After leaving the temple, buy two lances. We spend the night in the middle of the Nile.

Thursday, 4 April [*1850*]. Leave at 4 a.m. About eleven, we meet the *cange* of the effendi whom we had already seen at Wadi Halfa and who is the Nazir of Ibrim, charged with extorting taxes from Assuan to Wadi Halfa. He had seized an unsuspecting village sheik who had not paid a sou of the tax demanded; the old man was chained to the bottom of the boat; all we could see of him was his bare black head, shining in the sun. The effendi's *cange* keeps close to ours for a while, when he accosts us and our bows touch; a man hands over a small bleating sheep, a present from the effendi, who is clearly not sorry to be with us, in case of trouble. All day, in fact, we see men and women from rebellious villages following us, or rather following him, on the bank.

He pays us a long visit, we make him a present of a bottle of Cyprus wine and one of raki. The sheik will be taken to Derr, where after four or five hundred blows he will be left fastened to a certain large sycamore tree until someone goes surety for him.

We talk of the bastinado with the Nazir. When a man is to be killed, four or five blows suffice—his lower back and neck are broken; when he is only to be punished, he is beaten on the buttocks: four or five hundred blows is the usual number; five or six months are required for the healing—until the lacerated flesh falls away. The effendi laughed as he

(145)

added that last detail. In Nubia the bastinado is usually given on the soles of the feet. The Nubians greatly dread this punishment, since after it they are never able to walk again. After a three-hour visit, the Nazir leaves us. He has his *cange* land him at the house of a chief of the 'Abadheh Bedouins, with an enclosed garden and palms. We see a lot of people under a thick-trunked, low-growing tree: he is probably sitting there bickering with them.

That evening we pull up close to the temple of Maharraka, which we visit after dinner, by the light of the stars. They shine between the columns, overhead, and through openings in the ruins: a sailor lights us with his lantern.

[*5 April*]. *Friday morning*. Visit the temple. Was it a temple? A church?

... While Max takes his picture, Joseph, sitting beside me on the sand, tells me about his childhood and how he left his country. Two or three flocks of partridges fly past and alight further on. To the left, behind us, a short row of palms. Nice little black boy scuffling in the sand and making faces to amuse us. We leave after killing the sheep given us by the Nazir of Ibrim.

Dakkeh. Sandstone temple ...

Saturday morning, [*6 April*.] I buy the hair of two women, together with their hair-ornaments. The women being shorn weep, but their husbands, who do the shearing, make ten piastres per head. As we are about to leave, a man comes up and offers us another head of hair, which Max buys. This must have been distressing to the poor women, who seem to prize their hair greatly.

Girsheh. Sand . . . temple . . . An old man, clean, with a white beard, finally agrees to sell Maxime a flask of antimony. A man in white smoking a *chibouk* in his doorway, shakes hands with Joseph. Inside the house a slave-trader, sitting on his mat; to the left, above him, hangs a long iron chain—a professional item . . . At nightfall, reach Dendur. Temple . . .

Sunday, 7 [April 1850]. Stay at Dendur el-gharb because of contrary wind.

Monday, 8 April. Kalabsheh. The village is in the midst of the ruins of the outbuildings of the temple . . .

9 April. Quarter to six in the morning. Tafah. Two temples. One, completely inside the village, is used as a dwelling. Both small. People come bringing us milk, chickens, small baskets and shields made of crocodile and hippopotamus hide.

Kartassi. Nine in the morning . . . Temple ruins . . .

[10 April.] Wednesday morning. Debot. Temple . . .

Before we cast off, a flat-nosed negro sorcerer comes to tell our fortunes. In a shallow basket full of sand he draws circles, and then draws lines out from each circle. He predicts that I 'will receive two letters at Assuan, that there is an old lady who thinks about me constantly, that I had intended to bring my wife along on the trip but finally decided to come alone; that I want both to travel and to be at home, that in my country there is a very powerful man who is most kindly disposed towards me, and that on my return to my country I'll be showered with honors.'

When I reached the *cange* I saw Joseph standing waiting on the deck; he came over to me quickly.

'Do you know what is new, Signor?' he said. 'Here is a *strego* who claims he can read in the sand, and wants to tell your fortune.'

And in fact I saw, standing among the sailors, a black whose intelligent face bespoke great refinement; he came toward me, took my hand, kissed it, and stood motionless. I gladly consented to the experiment that Joseph proposed. Out from under his long blue robe the Nubian produced a small copper dish; he filled it with sand and sat down cross-legged beside the gunwale. I faced him.

He placed the palm of his right hand on the sand, drew a few crisscross lines in it, and speaking slowly, without raising his eyes, he said:

'Your spirit has no country, you sleep as soundly under a tent as in your own house; your heart is black, because those who dwell there are now in the trumpet of the angel, who will sound the Last Judgment; you expect to receive letters at Assuan, but there are none; you will get them only in Cairo; when you read them a great storm will arise in your breast and you will weep like a newborn babe; you will return to your country, where you were long ill; you will not stay there, for your feet itch as soon as you are at rest; you will do yet more traveling by dromedary.'

He stopped. Several things were true of what he had told me, but Joseph could have told them to him after learning them from my servant. Despite his horoscope, I did find letters at Assuan two days later; in Cairo I was indeed to receive terrible news.

'When am I to die?' I asked him.

He effaced the lines he had made, drew others, looked at them and answered:

'I do not know, but you will die a violent death in a hot country.'

That last prediction impressed me, because this was the third time in ten years that it had been made to me. What difference does it make, after all! God will call me when He thinks the time is ripe. Whether it be under the sun of the Orient or under the cloudy skies of France, what difference does it make? One sleeps as soundly in the sands of the desert as in the damp mud of our cemeteries.

I paid the sorcerer and the *cange* took off.*

In 1850 the temple of Isis and the other buildings on the mid-Nile island of Philae, an hour or so above Assuan by donkey along the shore or across a stretch of desert, had long been in ruins, but the island itself stood well above water. (Since one of the raisings of the first Assuan dam in the present century only the tops of the monuments have been visible.) It was Du Camp's idea to camp for several days on Philae, where there was much to photograph and squeeze, and whence they could send the cange *down through the First Cataract to Assuan and visit that town as they chose.*

FROM FLAUBERT'S TRAVEL NOTES

[*10 April 1850.*] We arrive at Philae about 5 p.m. I take Joseph to Assuan at once, via the desert. We are

* Du Camp died peacefully in Baden-Baden at the age of seventy-two.

armed to the teeth, for fear of hyenas; our donkeys keep up a good trot; a young boy of about twelve, charming in his grace and nimbleness and clad in a long white shirt, runs ahead of us carrying a lantern. The blue of the sky is dotted with stars—they are almost like fires—the sky is aflame—a real oriental night. An Arab, riding a camel and singing, came into view from the right, cut across our path and disappeared ahead of us.

At Assuan there is an enormous packet, but nothing for me; Augier's *Gabrielle* is the only thing with my name on it. Plenty of letters for Max and Sassetti: I took that very hard. We return [to Philae] at once via the villages along the Cataract, our little guide being afraid of the desert because of wild animals.

Flaubert was so distressed at receiving no mail at Assuan that he wrote to his mother: 'Perhaps no one thinks of me any more? Can the old proverb be true, "Les absents ont tort?" As for our trip, I'll tell you about that another time . . . I am too angry to collect my thoughts.' The lack of mail—it was two months since he had heard from her—seems to have put him into a rather severe depression, and one wonders whether that helped account, two days later, for his unaccustomed failure chez ces dames.

FROM FLAUBERT'S TRAVEL NOTES

Thursday, 11 [April 1850]. Our tent is set up on the east beach at Philae, where we are moored. Unexpected arrival of Mourier and [Doctor] Willemin, in white hats. Abdulla (former servant in Brochier's hotel) is with them, as well as the doctor from Assuan, who remains with the servants. Very bawdy lunch—we break up at three. A stroll on the other side of the river, towards the village of Bab.—To pose I climb to the top of the mosque Kelell-Rasun-Saba. Marvelous facial expressions and gestures of our old Farghali, explaining that he understands nothing about photography and that it isn't his job anyway.

Friday 12 April. Descent of the [First] Cataract. The *cange* is full of people, as when we ascended the Cataract; among those on board is a priest, who prays unceasingly, balanced precariously on the starboard gunwale. Anxious moment when the boat plunges ahead as the cable is being paid out—it bobs like a cork in a millrace.

By the time we reach Assuan, at noon, I am dying of hunger. Lunch at the café, with fried fish and dates. What a good lunch! Barber. We visit Willemin and Mourier's boat. Mourier is at the cat-house. We visit *ces dames*. Dog barking, children crying. A little girl spawned by some Englishman, with square forehead and blonde hair, whom Willemin takes in his arms saying over and over again, '*Ah beuh! Ah beuh!*'* Mourier's sweat. I can't. . . .

We return via the desert. Camped at Philae Saturday, Sunday and Monday [13, 14 and 15 April]. I don't stir from the island, and am depressed. What is it, oh Lord, this permanent lassitude that I drag about with me? It followed me on my travels, and I have brought it home! Deianira's tunic was no less completely welded to Hercules' back than boredom to my life! It eats into it more slowly, that's all.†

* French baby-talk.

† At some time, in a similar mood, Flaubert made an undated entry on the last page of one of his travel notebooks, likening and unlikening his accesses of depression to the midsummer rising of the Nile: 'Oh Nile! Like your waters my

Monday, [*15 April*.] Fierce *khamsin*. The clouds are red, the sky is covered, the hot wind blows sand over everything: suffocating, depressing. It must be ghastly in the desert.

What makes one indignant at Philae are the religious depredations—reminiscent of the stupidity of the *expurgata*. In the last room of the large temple, a charming Isis nursing Horus—one often sees casts of this; in the first court, a thousand charming details. In one of the upper rooms, scenes of embalming: in the corner to the right a woman on her knees lamenting, her arms raised in despair; here the artist's observation cuts through the ritual of the conventional form. Small temple of Athor: the finest thing in it is the famous inscription: 'A page of history must not be soiled,' and the notation: 'A page of history is ineradicable.'

Tuesday, [*16 April*.] Set off via the desert with five camels carrying all our enormous paraphernalia. Two stations where we stop to drink; at the second, a little dead mouse beside the big water-jar. Arrive at Assuan about the same time as Max, who came via the Cataract in a small boat.

———————

sadness overflows, and no one can say whence it comes. It was in the heart (the middle) of my summer that the flood came rushing, but nothing will grow on the silt that it leaves behind.'

On the back of that same page he writes quite differently, proclaiming himself the only person on the Nile who wonders about the widely divergent types of humanity traveling on the river, thinking their own thoughts: '. . . what is going on in all the *canges* that are fitted out like ours ? English . . . gentlemen with ladies—albums displayed on round tables—they will be talked about in green parks . . . and the negress in the harem will think of this sun, which . . . when she was dragged under the awning of the *cange* and went below, not knowing where she was being taken.'

Wednesday, 17 [April]. Stroll in Assuan. Buy a silver ring from a woman selling bread. These street-corner bread-sellers are usually former *almehs*. At Esna it was Bambeh who provided us with our bread. Sultan, a poor wretch, a wreck, devoured by syphilis; I have the idea of sending him to Cairo.

At sunset, a visit from *ces dames*, Azizeh and the small laughing one, and a third, tall, with expression-less face, pock-marked; the sailors watch us, and a crowd gathers, attracted by the sound of the *dara-bukehs*—all this is distracting. All the women have that movement of the head sliding on the vertebrae that so astonished us the first time. We go inside with them so that they can dance the Bee for us. But the Bee is a myth, a lost dance whose name alone survives. Joseph claims to have seen it really danced only once, and by a man. As for the present version, it consists of stripping and crying: '*In ny a oh ! In ny a oh !*' ('Watch out, the bee! Watch out, the bee!').

Du Camp combines Azizeh's two dancing exhibitions into one. As always in Le Nil, *he says nothing of his traveling companion, but here his presence is hinted at in the mention of the Rouen carving of the dancing Salome, which Flaubert knew well and which was to be part of his inspiration, along with Azizeh and others, for Salome's dance in the tale* Hérodias.

FROM 'LE NIL, EGYPTE ET NUBIE'
BY MAXIME DU CAMP

[*Assuan.*] One morning in the bazaar, under a roof of mere straw matting that filters the sun—there is many a tear made by the heads of passing drome-daries—I was sitting lunching on fresh fish and dates when an unveiled woman stopped beside me. She kissed my hand respectfully and said:

'I am a dancer; my body is suppler than a snake's; if you wish, I can come with my musicians and dance barefoot on the deck of your boat.'

'The *cawadja* has seen Kuchuk Hanem at Esna,' Joseph answered her.

'Kuchuk Hanem doesn't know how to dance,' she replied.

I told Joseph to accept; and towards evening, when the setting sun had tempered the heat and shadows spread over the river bank, the dancer came with her players of the *rebec* and the *darabukeh*.

She was a tall Nubian, born in Korosko, named Azizeh.

She is elegant, and almost awesome, with her black skin, like bronze in its nuances of green and copper; her crinkly hair, full of gold piastres, is barely covered by a yellow kerchief dotted with blue flowers; her markedly slitted eyes seem like silver globes inset with black diamonds, and they are veiled and languid like those of an amorous cat. Her white, even teeth glitter from behind the thin lips of her mouth; a long necklace of sequins hangs down to her belly, which is circled by a girdle of glass beads that I can see through the diaphanous folds of her clothing.

Her dance is savage, and makes one think involuntarily of the contortions of the negroes of central Africa. Sometimes she uttered a shrill cry, as though to spur the zeal of her musicians. Between her fingers her noisy castanets tinkled and rang unceasingly.

'*Cawadja*, what do you think of Kuchuk Hanem now?' she cried, as she writhed her hips.

She held out her two long arms, black and glistening, shaking them from shoulder to wrist with an imperceptible quivering, moving them apart with soft and quick motions like those of the wings of a hovering eagle. Sometimes she bent completely over backwards, supporting herself on her hands in the position of the dancing Salomé over the left portal of the Rouen cathedral.

All the sailors from the boats moored at Assuan, and the town loungers, and slaves and slave-traders, gathered opposite my *cange* and watched and applauded the strange dancer, who was proud of the admiration she aroused. When she had finished, and I paid her, and she left wishing me *bon voyage* and long prosperity, the crowd around us slowly dispersed; and then I saw a horrible monster climbing on board my boat, dragging himself up the plank that served as gangway for landing.

He crawled towards me, trying to speak, uttering hoarse grunts punctuated by moans that were like appeals for help. Thus he made his way to the divan where I was sitting, seized my hand, which I snatched away from him before he could touch it with his lips, and looked at me with the expression of a hurt dog asking for comfort from his master.

His twisted, ulcerated legs had become so enfeebled as barely to support him; his eyes were infinitely sad, and tears escaped from beneath their reddened, bloated lids; his lips were covered with sores, and with a whitish slobber; his throat was swollen and purple, crusted with blood; his thickened tongue was helpless beneath the shreds of his half-destroyed palate; his voice was but a series of hiccoughs mingled with sobs.

Ah! If, like Candide, I had 'inquired into cause and effect, and as to the sufficient reason that had reduced this wretch to such a piteous state,' he could have replied, like Pangloss, 'Alas—it was love—love, the consolation of the human race, the preserver of the universe, the soul of all sensitive beings—tender love!'

By an irony of fate, this unhappy victim of implacable Venus bore the name of a king, and was called Sultan Ahmed. A *raïs* who was leaving for Cairo agreed to convey him there, and three months later I saw him again, in the hospital of Kasr el-'Aini, rejuvenated, erect, and almost rid of his frightful sores. Egypt is a country created by Aesculapius—all sicknesses are cured there.

FROM FLAUBERT'S TRAVEL NOTES

Thursday, 18 [April 1850]. [Assuan.] In the morning the Governor of Assuan, and Malim Khalil and his son, and the Nazir of Ibrim came to see us, all of them hoping for a bottle of *raki*; we pay Malim Khalil an *ukkah** of tobacco. These people are all frightful *canaille*; their baseness is disclosed by all the marks of respect they are shown. Take steps about Sultan—obvious official obstructionism. When he learned that he would be leaving and could be cured, he tried to kiss our feet; he was moved to tears. Unmerited gratitude is embarrassing; it is the reward for something that hasn't cost one anything; one feels ashamed, and as though indebted to the one who feels indebted to you.

At six in the evening Hasanin breaks a leg while carrying a heavy plank; he drops like a wounded

---

* Almost three pounds. Who Malim Khalil was, and why he had to be paid, are not explained. Perhaps in connection with Sultan's departure.

bird. First aid on the sand by torchlight. All night we hear him moaning: '*Cawadja, cawadja!*'

Friday, 19 [April] . . . We carry Hasanin on board the *cange* and leave Assuan.

Saturday, 20 [April]. Kom Ombo. Arrive in the afternoon. The ruins of the temple go down to the Nile . . .

Monday, 22 April. Edfu. The temple of Edfu serves as public latrine for the entire village . . .

Wednesday, 24 [April]. El-Kab. Early morning, set out for the rock tombs . . . Nothing more amusing that these paintings, which get away from the pitiless rigidity of Egyptian art.

Friday, 26 [April]. Esna. Arrive at 6 a.m. Cloudy, oppressive weather, white sky.

About ten o'clock Bambeh comes aboard the *cange*; her right eye is sore and she keeps it covered with a scarf. We give her some lead acetate for it. The sheep is no longer with her; the sheep is dead. We go to Kuchuk Hanem's through back streets, Bambeh walking ahead.

At Kuchuk Hanem's. The house, the courtyard, the ruined stairs—they are all there, but she is not there—not at the top of the stairs, her torso bare in the sunlight! We hear her voice greeting Joseph; we go up to the first floor, Zeneb pours water on the pavement. Silence; the air is oppressive; we wait.

She comes in, no tarboosh, no necklace, bareheaded, her short braids all over the place; seen like this her head is very small above the temples. She looks tired, as though she has been sick. She puts a kerchief on her head, sends for her necklaces and earrings, which are in safe-keeping with a sharif of the town, as is her money: she keeps nothing in the house, for fear of thieves. We exchange courtesies and compliments. She has often thought of us; she thinks of us as her children; she has never met nicer *cawadjas*.

Two other women: the first, who has a long straight nose, sits down cross-legged on the left; the second is short, dark, quite pretty in profile, but a wretched dancer. Our old musician and another with a white beard, escorted by his wife, an old woman who plays the tambourine; she is a dancing teacher, and makes signs to the little dancer, indicating her dissatisfaction by marking time and showing the proper steps. Smiling expression—square-faced like an old white eunuch. She begins to dance; her dance is a dramatic pantomime, making one think of what ancient dancing must have been like.

Kuchuk dances. Movement of the neck leaving the body, like Azizeh; and her charming, old style step, one foot in front of the other.

The walls of her bedroom on the ground floor are decorated with two labels, one a picture of Fame bestowing wreaths and the other covered with Arab inscriptions. My moustache still displeases her: since I have a small mouth I shouldn't hide it. We take our leave, promising to return to say goodbye.

In the courtyard, a tall rascal with one eye covered by a scarf; he holds out his hand, saying '*ruffiano*' *— I give him three piastres.

* *i.e.* he claims to be Kuchuk Hanem's pimp.

The result of all this—infinite sadness; like the first time, she had perfumed her breasts with rose-water. This is the end; I'll not see her again, and gradually her face will fade from my memory.

Bazaars—I sit almost all afternoon in a café watching people—a funeral procession crosses the square.

[*26 April 1850*] [*Mailing date.*] [*Esna*]. We are in full summer. At six in the morning it is normally 20° Réaumur in the shade, and during the day about 30°. [68° and 86° Fahrenheit.] The harvest is long since in, and yesterday we ate a watermelon. And you, dear old darling? Are you at Croisset? Nogent? Paris? And the trip to England? Send me the longest letter you can—tell me about yourself, the life you are leading, everything that is happening.

... We ourselves are leading a splendid existence. The trip to Nubia is over, and our entire stay in Egypt is approaching its end. Now we are going down, by oar, this great river up which we were borne by our two white sails. We stop at all the ruins. We tie up the boat and go ashore. There is always some temple buried to its shoulders in the sand, partially visible, like an old dug-up skeleton. Gods with heads of ibises and crocodiles are painted on walls white with the droppings of the birds of prey that nest between the stones. We walk among the columns; with our palmwood sticks and our day-dreams, we stir up this old dust; through holes in the temple walls we see the incredibly blue sky and the full Nile winding in the middle of the desert with a fringe of green on each bank. *This is the essence of*

Egypt. Often there is a flock of black sheep grazing around us, and some naked little boy, agile as a monkey, with the eyes of a cat, ivory teeth, a silver ring in his right ear, and scars on his face—tattooing done with a red-hot knife. Other times there are poor Arab women covered with rags and necklaces, come to sell Joseph chickens, or gathering goat-dung by hand to feed their meagre fields. One marvelous thing is the light, which makes everything glitter. We are always dazzled in the towns—it is like the butterfly colors of an immense costume ball; the white, yellow or blue clothes stand out in the transparent air— blatant tones that would make any painter faint away.

As for me, I think about what I have always thought about—literature; I try to take hold of everything I see; I'd like to imagine something. But what, I don't know. It seems to me that I have become utterly stupid. In the temples we read travelers' names; they strike us as petty and futile. We never write ours; there are some that must have taken three days to carve, so deeply are they cut in the stone. There are some that you keep meeting everywhere—sublime persistence of stupidity.*

FROM FLAUBERT'S TRAVEL NOTES

Friday, 26 April. [Probably for Saturday 27.] [Esna.]
. . . Coptic Monastery of the Martyrs, one league from

* In *Le Nil* Du Camp, too, excoriates the defacers of temple walls, and its later editions contain an indignant footnote: 'The preceding lines have brought me bad luck. A facetious tourist who apparently read them has amused himself by inscribing my name, in large capital letters, on several temples in Egypt and Nubia. I protest against this profanation, and I beg readers of this book who may travel on the Nile in future to be good enough to rub out those inanities, which I am incapable of having committed.'

Esna ... Staying as a guest here is an Abyssinian priest on his way home from Jerusalem—tall, thin, almond-eyed, long aquiline nose, fine face, completely Indian type; he is weak-chested and has the look of those who die of the wasting sickness. He is unhappy here, misses his country; Egypt is a kind of hell for him. We speak of Abyssinia. The rage for emasculation really does exist there, as I had been told. In Abyssinia there are more than twenty kings. Recently the Abyssinians killed an entire Turkish garrison that was on the island opposite Massaoua. For Europeans, traveling in small groups in the mountains is dangerous, since they are covered with forests leased as elephant-hunting preserves. He talks a great deal about the low cost of food in Abyssinia. When we take our leave we express our longing to see our own countries, so distant one from the other. May God have returned him safely to his.* As for the common bond of Christianity, it seems to me to be non-existent; the true bond is that of language: this man is much more the Moslems' brother than mine.

... While we were away, Kuchuk Hanem and Bambeh called on us.

... *A rich man going home:* we see the Governor of Assiut leaving Esna on his way to sleep in the Government Palace. On horseback, with an escort, preceded by two men carrying torches. Only those two are visible, outlined against the wall by the blazing resin; all the rest move as darker shadows in the darkness of the night; particles of fire spiral upward and fall to the ground behind them.

---

* That sentence was added by Flaubert in his re-writing; but in *Le Nil* Du Camp wrote of the Abyssinian: 'The poor man didn't have two weeks of life left in him.'

Sunday morning, 28 [April]. We leave Esna early and make progress all day by oar despite the head-wind.

Monday, [29 April]. At eight-thirty in the evening we reach Luxor.

VIII

Thebes

After the 'Eureka! Eureka!' anecdote in his Souvenirs
Littéraires, *Du Camp goes on to say, about Flaubert in
Egypt: 'Through a strange phenomenon, the impressions
of that journey that he seemed to disdain returned to him
in totality and in full force when he wrote* Salammbô.
*But then Balzac was the same: he looked at nothing and
remembered everything.' The present reader, who has
been aware from the beginning of how far Flaubert
was from 'disdaining' the journey, and how untrue it
was that 'he looked at nothing,' can only welcome Du
Camp's 'seemed to disdain'—his apparent realization
that he had been misled for years—until the publication
of* Salammbô—*by his companion's depressions, home-
sickness, and lack of interest in such indispensables as
photography, squeezes, and the measuring of temples
with metric tape.*

*But even Flaubert's monument-boredom vanished
before the splendor of Thebes. The temple of Luxor, the
halls of Karnak, and, across the river, the painted
tombs and the other temples (Medinet Habu, the Ramesseum, etc.) revived his enthusiasm—though even here
his participation in squeeze-making was reluctant, and
the detailed descriptions he sometimes felt obliged to
write are dispensable. As always, it was his own experiences amidst the monuments and the Egyptian landscape that most interested him: as we saw at Esna, to*

him the vignette of a yellow cow poking her head into a temple is as noteworthy as the fact that the temple itself is 33 m. 70 long. This Theban section is chiefly a series of vignettes.

The modern traveler to Egypt will notice that there is no mention of the great Deir el-Bahri of Queen Hatshepsut. In 1850 it was still unexcavated.

FROM FLAUBERT'S TRAVEL NOTES

Arrival at Luxor. We arrived at Luxor on Monday, 30 [*sic*, for 29] April [1850], at 8.30 p.m. The moon was rising. We go ashore. The Nile is low, and there is quite a broad stretch of sand between the water and the village of Luxor; we have to climb the bank to see anything. On the bank, a short man accosts us and asks to be our guide. We ask him if he speaks Italian. '*Si, signor, molto bene.*'

The mass of the pylons and the colonnades looms in the darkness; the moon, just risen behind the double colonnades, seems to be resting on the horizon, low and round and motionless, just for us, and the better to illumine the horizon's great flat stretch.

We wander amid the ruins, which seem immense; dogs are barking furiously on all sides, and we carry stones or bricks with us.

Behind Luxor, towards Karnak, the great plain looks like an ocean; the Maison de France is dazzlingly white in the moonlight, as are our Nubian shirts; the air is warm, the sky streams with stars; tonight they take the form of semi-circles, like half-necklaces of diamonds with here and there a few stones missing. What wretched poverty of language! To compare stars to diamonds!

Luxor. The next day, Tuesday, we visit Luxor. The village can be divided into two parts, separated by the two pylons: the modern part, to the left, contains nothing old, whereas on the right the houses are on, in, or attached to the ruins. The houses are built among the capitals of columns: chickens and pigeons perch and nest in great [stone] lotus leaves; walls of bare brick or mud form the divisions between houses; dogs run barking along the walls. So stirs a mini-life amid the debris of a life that was far grander . . .

The Pylons. The cornice of the pylons is badly damaged; only the part inside the door survives. On the two sides of the door, two colossi buried to the chest . . . The obelisk, in perfect state of preservation, is against the left-hand pylon. White birdshit streaks down from the very top and forms a flat mass at the bottom, like a dribble of plaster. Birdshit is Nature's protest in Egypt; she decorates monuments with it instead of with lichen or moss. The obelisk that is now in Paris was against the right-hand pylon. Perched on its pedestal, how bored it must be in the Place de la Concorde! How it must miss its Nile! What does it think as it watches all the cabs drive by, instead of the chariots it saw at its feet in the old days ?*

* There had been great public interest in the shipping to France, and the erection in the center of the Place de la Concorde, of one of the two pink granite obelisks from the temple of Luxor. The obelisk had been taken down under the supervision of French naval officers and engineers, and transported to Paris on the French ship *Louxor*, in 1832. Flaubert, then eleven years old, had perhaps seen it while it was still on board; for on the way up the Seine from Le Havre to Paris the *Louxor* had stopped in Rouen, where it was much visited. (It had passed directly in front of the riverside house at Croisset—but in 1832 Flaubert was not yet living there.)

Du Camp, in *Le Nil*, as Romantic as Flaubert about the

The interior of the pylon is hard to climb; the stones are placed corner to corner, as in the corridors of the Pyramids. From the top we look down on Joseph in his white shirt calmly sitting on the matting outside the mosque. (There is a long platform there, or low terrace, covered with matting.) To climb to the top of the pylons we pass through the interior of the mosque, where a whole school of youngsters is twittering, sitting cross-legged and rocking back and forth; the teacher is reading aloud, chanting in falsetto. The stairs of the pylon come down directly into the interior of the mosque.

*The Garden of Prisse d'Avennes.** We visit the former garden of Prisse, now belonging to the sheik of the 'Ababdehs. A masonry trellis covered with vines; dwarf or small palms. Two or three negro servants are moving about, and bring us bouquets of oleander. When we start to leave, one negro puts his back against the door as a way of demanding *baksheesh*—consequently we give him nothing.

FROM 'LE NIL, EGYPTE ET NUBIE' BY MAXIME DU CAMP

[*Luxor*.] Beyond [the temple] stands a large house built in part of antique materials above a sanctuary of

---

separation of the two obelisks that had stood together at Luxor for three thousand years, prefers to personify the one that remains: 'Alone and desolate under the implacable sun, it seems to be longing for its absent brother,' etc.

* French Egyptologist (1807–79), who seven years earlier, in 1843, had extracted from the temple of Thutmosis III at Karnak, and shipped to Paris, an entire chamber whose walls are covered with the names of Pharaohs in relief (the 'Chamber of the Ancestors,' now in the Louvre).

Alexander the Great; its walls of whitewashed brick rest on broken drums of columns, pillars sawn in half, stones covered with inscriptions; this is the Maison de France. The naval officers who took part in the *Louxor* expedition were quartered here, and ever since it has belonged to the French government, to whom Mohammed Ali orally presented it. Behind it is a magnificent green garden, planted by our sailors. Date palms, mimosas, broad-leaved banana-trees, oleanders and lemon-trees provide deep shade; an Arabian jasmine diffuses its perfume, doves sing under its leaves. I often sat there for hours at a time, smoking my bubbling *narghile* and watching the golden beetles scurry through the grass.

Today a part of the colonnade of the temple of Luxor is walled off and used as a storehouse for wheat. This is where they fasten—by the ears— dealers convicted of selling short weight. The poor devils groan and stand on tiptoe, to lessen the pain as best they can. Incidentally, this is an excellent measure that we would do well to borrow from the Orientals: their ways are sometimes wiser than ours. It is very simple to execute: I have often seen it in Cairo.

When the seller of some commodity is accused of cheating on the weight or quality of his merchandise, the *cadi* [judge] summons him, questions him, and if he is found guilty sentences him to be exposed for a few hours in front of his shop. Two *shauwish* [police-men] seize him and take him to his place in the bazaar; they close the shutters, make him stand on two bricks, and nail his ears to his own house. That done, they re-move the bricks and the poor fellow is left all but hanging, resting on the very tips of his toes. The *shauwish* sit down beside him, smoke their pipes, and see that no one comes to his aid. Between the guards and their patient there often ensues a dialogue something like this:

'Hey, you, son of so-and-so,' says the *shauwish*, 'your ear is getting a little long—it's longer now than the ear of an Abyssinian donkey.'

'Oh, *aga* [constable], the *cadi* was wrong; by Mohammed (may the blessings of God be upon him!) you might put at least one brick under my feet.'

'Not so, oh dog of a thief! Your ear is going to have to drag on the ground, to bear witness against you at the Last Judgment.'

'Hey, *aga*, I have piastres in my pocket.'

'How many?'

'Alas, I have only two, for I am but a poor merchant, unjustly sentenced.'

'Ah, if you have only two piastres, that means your ear isn't long enough.'

The patient insists and offers a second price; the *shauwish* finally gives in and slips back the two bricks, thus greatly easing the pain. But as soon as a bey or a pasha comes into view the *shauwish* quickly pulls out the bricks, and the poor fellow is left hanging again until the important personage is out of sight.

That is a summary, brutal form of justice, I know; but it is often a good thing to resort to it. A thieving baker, strung up by his ears to his own closed bakery, would have a stronger effect on his rascally fellow-bakers than all the feeble sentences in our law-makers' repertory. If I were Prefect of Police, I would now and then order such an edifying spectacle, and let the philanthropists cry as they might.*

* Parisien bakers never had to endure Maxime Du Camp as Prefect of Police.

Karnak. The first impression of Karnak is that of a palace of giants. The stone grilles still existing in the windows give the scale of these formidable beings. As you walk about in this forest of tall columns you ask yourself whether men weren't served up whole on skewers, like larks. In the first courtyard, after the two great pylons as you come from the Nile, there is a fallen column all of whose segments are in order, despite the crash, exactly as would be a fallen pile of checkers. We return via the avenue of sphinxes: not one has its head—all decapitated. White vultures with yellow bills are flying over a mound, around a carcass; to the right three have alighted and calmly watch us pass. An Arab trots swiftly by on his dromedary.

Sunset at Luxor. At sunset I go off in the direction of the French garden, to a little creek made by the Nile; the water is perfectly smooth—a midge dipping its wings would ruffle it. Goats, sheep and buffalo come pell-mell to drink; kids suck at their mothers as the latter drink in the water; one of them has its teats tied in a bag. Women come to fetch water in great round vases that they put on their heads; when one herd or flock has gone, another takes its place; the animals bleat or low in different voices; gradually all move off; night falls; here and there on the sand an Arab says his prayers. The gray hills opposite (the Libyan chain) are overlaid with a bluish tone; over the water the atmosphere is tinged with purple; then that color fades and night comes.

First Night at Medinet Habu. After dinner we cross the Nile and go on foot to the hill of Medinet Habu to spend the night, hoping to get a hyena. We lie down under the stars (and such stars!) on our coats, in the midst of the stones. Joseph and the guides talk all night; the sheep we bought in a village (on this side of the Nile) is tied up, and the next day we find it unharmed.

At six in the morning we breakfast in the palace of Medinet Habu on milk and hard-boiled eggs. The hill, close behind, looms over this great building that still stands; architecture and landscape seem the work of the same hand.

Le Sieur Rosa. We pay a visit to Sieur Rosa, a dealer in antiquities, a Greek from Lemnos. This is carrying hatred of vegetation pretty far—the site of his house is a plaster-furnace. Dogs bark, no one wants to let us in; finally they open the door. In the courtyard, mummies stripped of their bandages standing in the corner to the left as you enter; one of them still has his hands on his phallus; another has a twisted mouth and hunched shoulders as though he had died in convulsions. In a low-ceilinged room on the ground floor, mummies in their coffins: very beautiful coffin of a woman, with painting in tones of brown; two other mummies in unopened coffins. The old Greek lives there; his eyes are diseased and he keeps wiping them with a handkerchief. We talk politics—that is, the situation in Greece; he goes to fetch Greek newspapers and reads a few passages in a very low voice.

The colossi of Memnon are very big, but as far as being impressive is concerned, no. What a difference from the Sphinx! The Greek inscriptions are very easily read; we had no trouble in making squeezes. Stones that so many people have thought about, that so many men have come to see, are a joy to look at. Think of the number of bourgeois stares they have received! Each person has made his little remark and gone his way.

Back to the *cange* about three o'clock.

Maison de France. We are going to sleep in the Maison de France. The stairs give on a rubbishy part of the village [of Luxor], with the brothels at the far end. We have two rooms. In the first there is a fireplace—Joseph goes there. Abdul-mineh (the house watchman) and the sailors on a mat. The small room for photography is on the right; our bedroom, with divan, to the left, with a balcony giving on the Nile. View on to the mountains of the Libyan chain. Visit to the Governor about the business of the sheik at Kurna.* In the afternoon, ride to Karnak (on a saddle that ruins my arse) to mark the squeezes that are to be made. In the evening the Governor returns our visit.

Saturday morning, [*4 May*]. Stroll in Luxor. Café. Amiable, pleasant Turks. Albanian soldiers playing with small shells in a kind of hollow checkerboard; one Albanian tries to ride his horse up a flight of stairs. Turk in red jacket who offers me a drink of *bouza.*

We leave for Karnak. Lodged in the King's Chamber, once occupied by Dr Lepsius. Small green pond where every night there sails a gold *cange* with gold men; edged with sharp prickly reeds. Maxime bathes in it. The look of his naked body, standing on the edge.

* The sheik of the village of Kurna, across the Nile, had raised some objection about squeezes, which they had apparently made without his permission.

I spend the night outside, on a mattress laid on a stone, wearing only my Nubian shirt. Gloriously scintillating stars. Guards. One above me, whom I catch sight of during the night. Jackals bark frightfully and in great numbers. The clicking sound made by tarantulas. During the night jackals come to eat our supplies.

FROM 'LE NIL, EGYPTE ET NUBIE' BY MAXIME DU CAMP

[*Karnak.*] Near my room, amid thickly-growing reeds, there was a small round pond full of salamanders, which was formerly the sacred basin for ablutions. It was into this pond, according to a still-preserved Coptic tradition, that the Egyptian priests cast the gold and silver ornaments of the temples of Karnak at the time Cambyses sacked the city of Thebes. My guide, Temsah, told me in a low voice that every night one could see, afloat on the thick, muddy water of this lake, a gold boat steered by silver women and drawn by a great blue fish. Many Arabs have tried to lay hands on it, but the enchanted boat vanished in smoke as soon as anyone came near.

FROM FLAUBERT'S TRAVEL NOTES

Sunday, 5 [May 1850.] Superintend squeezes in the palace. When that stupid job is done, walk around Karnak.

... In the evening an effendi, a local land-owner, comes to pay us a visit; he is dressed in white, is letting his beard grow, seems to be very hot—wide shirt-sleeves; he keeps stroking his arms with his hands; fat hands and feet. On my right his black servant sits cross-legged, holding a lance; his rifle is in the corner, a *yataghan* in his belt.

Monday. More squeezes. The means destroys the end; a good idling in the sun is less sterile than these occupations that one doesn't put one's heart into.

... In the evening our friend the effendi paid us another visit. He is from Baghdad, likes us very much, and accepts, 'for his father,' a box of cantharides pills. During the day he had sent us presents of milk, chickens, and a sheep. His little negro: damask jacket, round bulging eyes slightly bloodshot.

Medinet Habu ... On the left, entrance to the palace ... In the first court ... Second court ... East side ... North side ... Third court ...

While we are loading everything, to go on to the Ramesseum, one of our camels goes berserk and races off across the fields; his load falls off piece by piece; he puts his foot into a metal pitcher, which rides on his leg like a bracelet. Brochier's table is smashed to pieces.

[*Ramesseum.*] Hypogea or syrinxes. [Apparently the rock tombs in the slopes above the temple.] This is incontestably the most curious aspect of Egyptian art. Depiction of trades, etc. Mandolin-players—the neck of the mandolin very long; flute-players, harpists; naked whores—deliberately lubricious aspect of the thighs, with the knee deeply inset; *ces demoiselles* are clad in transparent dresses, recalling Devéria's* brothel scenes of 1829. So dirty pictures existed even so far back in antiquity ?

* Achille Devéria, French engraver, 1805–57.

. . . Whole families live in these tombs, with their naked children, chickens, etc. Some of them have fashioned doors from ancient painted coffin-lids.

From there, the ground under your feet is riddled with holes, like a sieve, and frightfully so. The Plain of Thebes. In the middleground, the two colossi seen from behind; Medinet Habu to the right, standing out distinctly in the plain . . . Beyond the plain, the blue Nile; then Luxor, incomparable in its effect of ruins in a landscape . . . In the left background, Karnak, a confused mass . . .

Kurna . . . Acrimonious visit from the sheik, on the subject of our squeezes in the small tomb.

Biban el-Muluk. We leave Kurna for the Valley of the Kings. White earth; sun; one's rump sweats in the saddle . . . We are camped at the entrance of the tomb marked No. 18 . . . Arabs stretched on the ground talking in low voices. Sassetti asleep on the pile of rugs. Max gone to explore Belzoni's Tomb.

Gargar. Gargar, old, dry and robust, lover of *raki* and bardashes. According to him, one can be strong only if one drinks brandy; that is why Franks are superior to Moslems. To prove this he gives himself great blows on the chest and knocks down several of the other Arabs. Once they're down he pretends to bugger them. He asks us to give his greetings to the officials in Luxor, whom he greatly likes.

Hyena-hunters. The look of the hyena-hunters. The old one—short, gray beard, smiling, wearing good red shoes; his companion, a man of thirty-six, sandals, matchlock rifle; a somber personage, more frightening to meet than his prey. They carry a small leather water pouch, which is their only provision for three or four days; when they kill a hyena they eat it and take the skin. The bad state of our shoes forces us to renounce this shooting expedition, which would have been very curious.

All the time I am at Medinet I am given as groom a little girl, ten or twelve years old, whose duty it is to follow my horse even though it should trot or gallop— which means that I always have to *walk* my horse. Can it be that parents in this country are even stupider than in ours?

Tomb of Merenptah . . . Tomb No. 16 . . . Tomb No. 9 . . . Left Biban el-Muluk Sunday, 12 [May].

Monday, 13 [May 1850] . . . Once again we pass through Karnak, along the southern edge of the little green pond. I long to see our little room again, and the stone I slept on under the stars. Karnak seems to me more beautiful, more grand, than ever. Sadness at leaving *stones*! Why?

FLAUBERT TO HIS MOTHER

Between Kuft and Kena.
17 May 1850. 1 p.m.

We finally (and alas!) left Thebes yesterday morning. It is a place where one could stay a very long time and in a perpetual state of astonishment. It is by far the finest thing we have seen in Egypt, and perhaps will remain the high point of our entire trip. Tonight we shall probably reach Kena. If I have no letters there, there is no hope of any before Cairo. God bless the mails, and the people at the consulate! If I at least knew that you were getting mine!

(175)

... From Kena we are going to make a sortie as far as Koseir, to see the Red Sea, which we would otherwise miss, as our projected trip to Sinai has been abandoned. For that we would have had twenty days of desert (in the month of July it might be strenuous), plus twelve days' quarantine in the lazaretto at Gaza and three thousand francs passage-money to the Sheik of 'Akaba; it would be absurd. Whereas the trip to Koseir will take only four or five days—a mere stroll.

... I thought constantly of Alfred [Le Poittevin] at Thebes. If the system of the Saint-Simonians is true, he was perhaps traveling with me, and it was not I who was thinking of him, but he thinking in me. And I often think of *the Others*, too, my darling! I cannot admire in silence. I need to shout, to gesticulate, to expand; I have to bellow, smash chairs—in other words I want others to share in my pleasures. And what others would I want but those I love best?

... When I take a sheet of paper to write you, I have no idea of what I am going to say. Then it begins to come of itself, and I find myself chattering away. I enjoy it; line follows line. And when I have no more to say I read it over, as a sort of farewell, and whisper to it in my thoughts: 'Go quickly! Kiss her for me!' Lines of handwriting kissing! Am I not silly? Let's not overdo it!

MAXIME DU CAMP TO MADAME FLAUBERT

(Written on a page of the preceding)
Chère Madame: Let me too send you a word of remembrance and of very positive assurance about Gustave's excellent health. He keeps faithfully to his diet, and Dr Cloquet's advice is followed exactly. I

hope that you will have only cause for self-congratulation about this long journey. It is fine and warm, usually from 33° to 37°; the young man perspires profusely; his beard reaches his waist. He is dark as a mole and eats like a wolf. I am very sorry that you cannot see for yourself the way we travel; it is one long promenade. The greatest hardship is having occasionally to sleep on a rug. As for safety, one goes everywhere here with one's hands in one's pockets; the peasants greet you respectfully as they pass. Do not worry in the least; write as often as you can . . .

FLAUBERT TO HIS MOTHER
(Postscript to the above)

18 May. Kena.

Joy! Joy! My heart is leaping with it. *Ten* letters for me, including one from Uncle Parain and one from Bouilhet. I will answer them soon. I smother you with kisses. I see that you are well, that you are being sensible! I love you a thousand times the more for that. How darling your letters are! I devoured them like a starving man. Adieu—in my next I'll speak to you about everything you mention. Don't worry about me—a thousand more kisses!

IX

To the Red Sea

In November, *a short Romantic novel composed before he was twenty-one and published only posthumously, Flaubert had written about desert travel out of his imagination and reading:*

'*Oh, to be bending forward on a camel's back! Before you a deep red sky and deep brown sand, the flaming horizon stretching ahead, the undulating ground, the eagle hovering above your head, in one part of the sky a flock of rosy-legged storks passing over on their way to the cisterns. The ship of the desert lulls you; the sun makes you close your eyes, bathes you in its rays. All you hear is the muffled tread of the animals. The leader has just ended his song; we ride and ride, on and on. At evening stakes are planted, tents pitched, the dromedaries are watered; we stretch out on a lion skin, we smoke, we light fires to keep off the jackals we hear barking in the depths of the desert. Unknown stars, four times the size of ours, throb in the skies. In the morning the water-skins are refilled at the oasis; we set off again; we are alone; the wind whistles and the sun rises in whirling clouds.*'

In memory of the young Flaubert, one is tempted to go on:

'*And then, on some plain where we gallop all day, palms grow between pillars; their branches wave softly beside the still shade of ruined temples. Goats climb on*

*the fallen pediments and munch the weeds that have
flourished in the marble carvings; they leap off in flight
when you approach. Then, after passing through forests
of trees linked by gigantic lianas, after crossing rivers
so broad their farther bank is not to be seen, you come
to the Sudan, the land of negroes, the land of gold. But
on! Still further! I long to see furious Malabar and
its dances of death: the wines are as deadly as poison,
the poisons as sweet as wine; the sea, a blue sea full of
pearls and coral, re-echoes the clamor of the sacred
orgies celebrated in the mountain caves. There is not a
wave stirring, the air is silver-gilt, the cloudless sky is
mirrored in the warm ocean; hawsers steam when they
are drawn out of the water, sharks follow the ship and
batten on the dead. Oh India! India above all!' Etc.*

Flaubert's journal of his trip across the desert to
Koseir, on the Red Sea, provides us with a later, real-
life parallel narrative. The pair form a pendant to his
two descriptions of the view from the top of the Pyramid.

FROM FLAUBERT'S TRAVEL NOTES

Thursday, 16 May [1850]. Kena. Our *cange* pulls up
on the beach at Kena ... The entire day and the next
are devoted to preparations for the trip to Koseir ...
Long lunch with Père Issa, discussing the price of the
desert crossing ... We buy waterskins, which we
shall wash in the small branch of the Nile behind
Kena.

FROM 'LE NIL, EGYPTE ET NUBIE'
BY MAXIME DU CAMP

[*Kena.*] Following various streets, and finally the
Street of the Scholars, I soon found myself before a

good-sized house, and went in: it was the home of the French consular agent in Kena. He is a Christian from Bethlehem called Issa, fairly intelligent and very obliging to travelers. In one of the rooms of his house I saw a kind of platform, covered with shawls and surmounted by a crucifix, which serves as altar for the Catholic Christians of the town and its environs. Issa gave me an excellent dinner, and immediately turned his attention to the business on which I had come. I wanted to go to Koseir, on the shore of the Red Sea; I had four days of desert-crossing to do and I was applying to the agent to procure the dromedaries and guides I needed. Joseph hardboiled some eggs, bought some goatskin 'water-bottles,' some bread, tobacco and *kamr-ed-din* (a kind of apricot paste imported from Syria and very useful while traveling), two bottles of *raki* and some *khordja* (large tasseled saddle-bags for camels).

That same evening the camel-drivers appeared with their animals and spent the night beside the *cange*; and the next day, wearing for comfort's sake clothing *à la* Nizam*—that is, gaiters, wide baggy trousers, belt and jacket—I was ready to set out.

FROM FLAUBERT'S TRAVEL NOTES

Saturday, 18 May. We rise at dawn; drawn up on the beach are four slave-traders' boats. The slaves come ashore and walk in groups of fifteen to twenty, each led by two men. When I am on my camel, Hadji-Ismael runs up to give me a handshake. The man on the ground raising his arm to shake the hand of a man mounted on his camel, or to give him something, is one of the most beautiful gestures of the Orient;

* The Egyptian regular infantry.

especially at the moment of departure there is something solemn and sad about it. The inhabitants of Kena are not yet up; the almehs, decked with golden piastres, are sweeping their doorways with palm branches and smoking their morning chibouk. The sun is dim, veiled by the *khamsin*. On the left, the cliff-like Arabian hills; ahead, the grayish desert; on the right, green plains. We follow the desert's edge, gradually leave the cultivated plain behind: it drops away to the right, and we plunge into the desert. After four hours we arrive at a small grove of *gassis* in which stands a long, one-storey building with an arcaded gallery; it is a *khan*, Bir 'Ambar. There we eat lunch, sitting on mats . . . , and take our siesta.

Reach Bir 'Ambar 9.30; leave 11.30.

Facing the arcade of the *khan* [caravansary], two long stone troughs where the camels are watered. Arabs in the shade, eating, praying, sleeping; the animals, like the humans, are under the trees, grouped haphazardly: the authentic 'Travelers' Rest.'

The terrain is rolling and stony, the trail arid, we are in full desert, our camel-drivers sing, and their song ends with a half-whistling, half-guttural modulation meant to excite the dromedaries. Visible on the sand are several tracks that wind parallel: these are caravan trails—each track was made by a camel. Sometimes there are fifteen to twenty such tracks; the wider the trail, the more numerous they are. Here and there, about every two or three leagues (but irregularly spaced), large plaques of yellow sand that look as if they were varnished with *terre-de-Sienne*—colored laqueur; these are the places where the camels stop to piss. It is hot; on the right a *khamsin* dust-cloud is moving our way from the direction of the Nile (of which all that we can faintly see now is a few of the palms that line the bank). The dust-cloud grows and comes straight at us—it is like an immense vertical cloud that before enveloping us is already high above us for some time, while its base, to the right, is still distant. It is reddish brown and pale red; now we are in the midst of it. A caravan passes us coming the other way; the men, swathed in *kufiyehs* [head-cloths] (the women are thickly veiled) lean forward on the necks of their dromedaries; they pass very close to us, no one speaks; it is like a meeting of ghosts amid clouds. I feel something like terror and furious admiration creep along my spine; I laugh nervously; I must have been very pale, and my enjoyment of the moment was intense. As the caravan passed, it seemed to me that the camels were not touching the ground, that they were breasting ahead with a ship-like move-ment, that inside the dust-cloud they were raised high above the ground, as though they were wading belly-deep in clouds.

From time to time we meet other caravans. One first sees them as a long horizontal line on the horizon, barely distinguishable from the horizon itself; then that dark line rises above the other, and on it one begins to make out small dots; the small dots them-selves rise up—they are the heads of camels walking abreast, swaying regularly along the entire line. Seen foreshortened, they look like the heads of ostriches.

The hot wind comes from the south; the sun looks like a tarnished silver plate; a second dust-spout comes on us. This one advances like the smoke from a conflagration, suet-colored, with jet-black tones at the base: it comes . . . and comes . . . and the curtain is on us, bulging out in volutes below, with deep black fringes. We are enveloped by it: the force of the wind is such that we have to clutch our saddles to stay on.

When the worst of the storm has passed, there comes a hail of small pebbles carried by the wind: the camels turn their tails to it, stop, and lie down. We resume our way.

Towards 7.30 in the evening the dromedaries abruptly change their course and head south. A few moments later we spy in the darkness a few low-lying hovels with dromedaries sleeping around them; it is the village of Lakeita. There is a well here, good for camels. Ten or so shapeless huts built of piled-up dry stones and straw mats, inhabited by 'Ababdehs. A few goats are hunting for a bit of grass between the stones, pigeons are pecking at the remains of the camels' straw, vultures strut around the huts. No one will sell us milk. A negress's teat—it hangs down well below her umbilicus, and so flat that it is scarcely the thickness of the two layers of skin; were she to go on all fours, it would certainly trail on the ground.

We sleep on our blankets on the ground. At three I awake; we leave at five, going on foot for the first hour.

In the middle of the day we stop for four hours at Gamseh Shems, in a small cave formed by a fallen rock; I lie down there on my back. When I raise my hand (stretching as I wake) the heat of the wind on it is like the breath of an oven; we have to wrap our hand-kerchiefs around the pommels of our saddles. Toward four o'clock, on the right, in the black rock, hiero-glyphs overlaid with Greek inscriptions: sacrifice to Ammon the Begetter and to Horus. The space be-tween the hills gradually narrows; we are walking in a wide corridor. In the evening, beautiful moon: the shadows of our camels' collars sway on the sand. At half-past nine we pass close to a large structure within a square walled enclosure; it is the well of Bir Hammamat, dug by the English. We push ahead and spend the night half an hour further on, after a march of eleven hours.

Monday, *20* [*May*]. Set out at half-past four. Mountain defile, up and down. In the middle of the trail, at a place where the mountains draw apart, a dead *gassis* stripped of its bark; a few other, small ones, in bloom, further on. One of our two camel-drivers takes an empty waterskin and runs on ahead of us; a good hour later we find him at Bir es-Sidd (Well of the Lock, Closed Well). This is an excavation in the earth, three feet in diameter, reached by sliding under a rock. There is little water, and what there is is very earthy; it is at an extremely narrow stretch of the trail as you come from Kena—after it, the trail climbs. Down by the well, ten paces before it, we find an old Turk, calmly sitting there on a rug with his servants and his wives. Beside the well, a camel lying on its side and uttering its death-rattle; it broke its back falling into the well, its owner pulled it out, and it has remained there, dying, for three months. When its owner passes he feeds it, and Arabs give it water to drink; the great number of *hadjis* [pilgrims] passing by explains why it hasn't been devoured by wild beasts.

While we were there, a caravan arrives from the opposite direction: the gorge is very narrow; congestion of camels and people; everyone has to dismount and lead his camel by the halter. We go on foot for a time because of the difficulty of the trail: it is strewn with the carcasses of camels; they have their skins, but are completely gutted. This is the work of rats: the hide, dried and stretched by the sun, is intact, but has been gnawed from within until it is no thicker than an onion-skin; it covers the skeleton, which is itself scarred with scratches made by the rodents' teeth. Innumerable rat-holes in the desert.

The trail broadens again, we pass close beside a demolished *khan*, Okkel Zarga (Purple Khan). Not a sound, devouring heat, one's hands tingle as in the hot-room of a bath . . . At quarter to twelve we take shelter beneath a large pink granite rock, where a flock of desert partridges were enjoying the cool; this place is called Aby Ziram (Father of the Jars). We gobble a watermelon that Joseph bought this morning at Bir es-Sidd; we have to abandon our chickens—gone bad. The day before, at the same time, we had to throw away our leg of lamb; scarcely had it fallen to the ground when a vulture fell on it and began to devour it. All day we keep seeing large numbers of partridges.

In the evening, Joseph's camel bolts. I see it pass by on my left. Joseph terrified and shouting; his white jacket disappears into the night. We make haste to follow after him, more especially as our camels show signs of imitating his. It comes back to us at a walk. We pass ropes through the nostrils of our dromedaries, who are trembling and in a rage: we prudently stop, and spend the night in a very beautiful open spot—a kind of small plain opening out to our left in the hills of Daoui (Clear or Open Place).

Tuesday, 21 [May]. Set out at 4 a.m., descending steadily. Many more caravans; the hills are now white, with long dark streaks. At eight we reach Bir el-Beida (White Well, because of the nearby mountains), or Bir el-Inglis (Well of the English, who dug it). 'Ababdehs are encamped around the well. Hovels of straw mats and earth. This is an open place, a plain in the midst of mountains. A young man, naked except for cotton drawers, his skin gray with dirt or dust, takes my camel (gesture of his raised arm as he leaps up!) to give it a drink; he draws water into a skin at the end of a rope and pulls it up, full, or almost full, and pissing from all its holes. The well is enclosed within a curb of dry stones, wide at the base and slanting: he braces his foot against it as he draws. The camels drink slowly and in huge amounts: it is three days since they drank last. We are thirsty too, and the water is execrable. The 'Ababdehs refuse to sell us milk, their only food.

The trail bends to the left; we descend. The chalky mountains surrounding this plain recall the Mokattam. The sky is full of clouds, the air humid, one feels the sea, our clothes are moist. I long to be there; it is always the same whenever I am nearing a goal: I have patience in all things—as far as the antechamber. A few drops of rain. An hour after leaving the well we come to a place full of reeds and high grass; dromedaries and donkeys are in the midst of it, eating and enjoying themselves. Water flows at the roots of the grass in numerous small streams, which deposit considerable quantities of salt on the ground; this is Wadi Ambagi (Place Where There is Water). The hills subside, we turn to the right. A flat face of reddish rock, to the left, at the entrance to the broader valley which leads, first over stones, then over sand, to Koseir. In my impatience I go on foot, running over the gravel and climbing hillocks, hoping to see the sea a minute sooner. How often in the past I have eaten my heart out with impatience, as pointlessly as now! Finally I see the dark line of the Red Sea against the gray horizon. The Red Sea!

I remount my camel, and we proceed over the sand to Koseir. It is as though wind had blown the sea-sand back into this broad valley: it is like the abandoned bed of a gulf. From a distance we see the forward masts of ships . . . Birds of prey are flying about and perched on low sand-dunes. Sea and ships to the right; Koseir ahead, with its white houses. To the right, before turning, a few palms enclosed within white walls: a garden! What a blessing for the eyes!

We cross the town: our drivers take the halters and lead us; Arabs draw back on each side of the street to let us pass. We put up in the house of Père Elias, brother of Issa, of Kena. He is a Christian from Bethlehem, an old man with a white beard, open and cordial expression, the French agent in this town. On his doorstep we find M. Barthélemy , . . . attaché in the consulate at Jidda; he is untidily dressed and wears a straw hat covered with a white cotton cloth. We are installed in a small square pavilion, one window on the sea, another on the street, a third on Père Elias's courtyard, full of sacks of grain. The sea, seen from my window, is more green than blue. The Arab boats, with their outsize sterns, their frail bows and their high prow. Arrival of M. Métayssier, French consul at Jidda—his head sunk between his shoulders and giving off a musky smell, which makes me suppose that he wears a drain in his neck: garrulous, insipid, deadly, knows everything and everybody—has given advice to Casimir-Périer, to Thiers, to Louis-Philippe. Poor man! My journey wasn't yet over when I heard of the end of his: he died at Jidda after being there three months!

We make a tour of the town; it is quite clean—no longer like Egypt. Various races of negroes—some of the men look like women, especially one whom I saw on the wooden jetty . . . he had the breasts, thighs and buttocks of a woman, and his skull narrowed so sharply above the temples that it was almost pyramidal. There are, I think, even more varieties in the negro race than in the white. Compare the negro of the Senaar (Indian type, Caucasian, European, pure black) with the negro of Central Africa; the head of the negro from Guinea is a head of Jupiter beside it.

These people, naked and carrying a bowl (a hollowed-out calabash) as their only possession, come from heaven knows where; there are some who have been on the march for several years. Dr Rüppel saw some in the Kordofan who had been traveling for seven years; MM. Barthélemy and Métayssier, coming from Kena to Koseir, found one half dead from thirst on the way: he had been traveling in the desert for a year. Some come with their wives, who give birth en route. Tartars from Bukhara, in fur caps, ask us for alms; they have the faces of frightful scoundrels, especially one with two missing front teeth and a smile. We see them again later in the shade of a boat, sewing their rags. The pilgrims persecute you with their begging and crowd like famished vultures around watermelon rinds, which are devoured here down to the green. Certain negroes excessively tall and no less extraordinarily thin; they seem to be nothing but bones, and extremely weak: still one more kind of negro. The pearl-fishers' *pirogues*, which are dug-out tree-trunks; oars that are mere poles with a circular board nailed on the end. We walk along the shore, past the boats drawn up on the beach; some are made of a kind of Indian wood, yellow, very hard; all are held together with iron nails. Pitilessness of M. le Consul, who insists on prolonging the walk 'just for half an hour'; I am harassed by him and by fatigue. Of all wild beasts, one of the most dangerous is the man who likes to 'take a walk.'

Copious dinner, execrable water—and I had looked forward to slaking my thirst at Koseir! Everything is permeated by this ghastly odor of soap and rotten eggs, even the latrines, which smell of Koseir water and nothing else! Even adding a little *raki* doesn't help. M. Elias's son does not dine with us: he is a young man of about twenty, with a timid, pious look, pointed nose and pinched mouth. We are served by a young eunuch of about eighteen, Saïd, in a striped colored jacket: bare-headed, wavy hair, a small dagger stuck in his shawl-belt, bare arms, thick silver ring on one finger, pointed red shoes. His soft voice when he held out the coffee tray with his right hand, put his left hand on his hip, and said '*Tafaddal*' ['*S'il vous plaît*']. He has as fellow-servant a long imbecile named Abdallah, dressed in rags, whose intelligence isn't even up to snuffing the candles. How well I slept that night, on Père Elias's divan! What a delicious thing to rest one's body!

Wednesday, 22 [*May*]. Stroll in the town. The cafés are big *khans*, or rather *okkels*; they are empty during the day, then they gleam with the lighted *sheeshehs* of the pilgrims to Mecca. We visit the boat the pilgrims are to take . . . These Red Sea boats are terrifying: they reek of the plague; to step on board is frightening; thank God I don't have to sail in one. For latrines, there is a kind of wooden balcony, or armchair, fastened outside the gunwale: if the sea were a bit rough one would inevitably be washed away. The divan and cabin are in the poop—they have no flooring and are filled with freight. Men playing cards with little leather disks printed in color—there were suns, swords, etc. In the evening, at sunset, we swim. What a swim! How deliciously I lolled in the water!

Thursday. 23 [May]. We set out very early on donkeys to see Old Koseir, of which absolutely nothing remains. We are accompanied by M. Barthélemy, by Elias's son, who wears an ample brown robe that flaps in the wind and who rides his dromedary expertly, and by M. Métayssier's janissary, Reschid. He is a Kurd, was taken prisoner in the Hejaz and made to work water-wheels for seven years. His only ambition is to see Paris and enlist in the African service. He is madly in love with a woman he is taking with him to Jidda; he had already sent her away once for misconduct, but when he passed through Kena, where she was a prostitute, he took her back. He carries an arsenal on him and is pleased to take charge of our two rifles . . . M. Métayssier's second janissary, Omar Agas, tall, thin-faced, more intelligent than the other, blue robe. At Old Koseir the sea takes on fabulous colors, with no transition between them—from dark brown to limpid azure. The Red Sea looks more like the ocean than like the Mediterranean. So many shells! Maxime, who is suffering from indigestion, falls asleep on the sand. M. Barthélemy and young Elias look for shells. Smell of the sea. Large birds fly past, wings outspread. Sun, sun, and blue sea; in the sand, large pieces of mother-of-pearl.

At 4 o'clock we say goodbye to Père Elias: it was one of the moments of my life when I felt the saddest: my heart was heavy. Père Elias felt it himself: tears were in his eyes, and he kissed me.

Slept at El-Beida. I am the only one who eats—
Max has his indigestion and Joseph is feverish.
Violent gale all night.

Friday, 24 May. The water from Koseir, gone from
bad to worse in the skins, becomes undrinkable: we
have to make do with watermelons. We meet pilgrims
from Alexandria going to Koseir, all by dromedary;
the women are shouting, arguing, gesticulating. At
10 o'clock we stop in full sun in a wide plain, El-
Mour; we tie our blankets to a *gassis* as best we can
and try to sleep under them. In the evening, at a
quarter to eight, we stop and sleep at El-Markar
(The Cave).

Saturday, 25 [May]. At Bir es-Sidd. The poor
camel is dead and partly eaten: vultures keep a greedy
watch. I dip my face in a wooden bowl and swallow
great gulps of the well-water—earthy, but far prefer-
able to what we have in our waterbags. At half-past
ten we sleep on the steps of the big well of Bir el-
Hammamat. At eight we stop and pass the night at
Kasr el-Banat (Castle of the Maidens), despite the
remarks of our drivers, who tell us it is a place haunted
by the devil and dangerous to stop at. During the
night a jackal makes off with part of our stores that we
had left out to cool.

Sunday, 26 [May]. Set out at quarter to four in the
morning. Lunch at Lakeita—we eat watermelon.
The old woman who sneaks in and gathers up the
rinds. We go on without siesta.

At four in the afternoon we reach Bir 'Ambar.
Joseph has been delirious for the last three hours.
We lie down under some *gassis*, in the shade, and

drink our fill—drink till we are drunk. Horses, donkeys, camels and chickens make so much noise that our night is disturbed.

Monday, 27 [May]. At a quarter to four in the morning, we set out for Kena. After two hours we begin to meet large numbers of people and sight the square pigeon-cotes of Kena. At eight we reach the *cange*, where we are given a warm welcome. Hadji Ismael is the first to greet me, as he was the last to say goodbye.

From Kena to Koseir, 45½ hours' walking time; return, 41¼.

Go into Kena. I am exhausted. Bath. An *almeh* (Mère Maurice)—dark eyes, much lengthened by antimony; her face held up by velvet chinstraps; sunken mouth, jutting chin, smelling of butter, blue robe. She lives at the end of the street, in the last house. I see Hosna et-Taouilah again, who tells me in sign language that I have beautiful eyes and especially beautiful eyebrows. Like all *ces dames* in Egypt, she dislikes my moustache.

FROM THE SOUVENIRS LITTERAIRES
OF MAXIME DU CAMP

During this little expedition there occurred a painful incident between Flaubert and me, the only one of our entire trip: we did not speak to each other for forty-eight hours. It was both unpleasant and comical, for in this case Flaubert obeyed one of those irresistible impulses that sometimes overcame him. Besides, in the desert one is hypersensitive, as the story will show. We had left Koseir with three skins full of execrable water, which were to supply our needs on the way; all three skins were incautiously loaded on the same side of the same camel: on its other side was part of our baggage as counterweight. The desert is inhabited by a prodigious number of rats, who feed off dead animals and are troglodytes. They dig tunnels and hole up in them. The camel carrying our water supply put his foot down on a spot just above one of these tunnels: the earth gave way under its weight, the poor animal broke its leg, fell, and in falling tore the three waterskins. That happened the evening we left. We had three days to go before reaching the Nile, and two and a half before Bir 'Ambar, the only well on the way with water fit to drink.

On our way to Koseir we had found that Bir el-Hammamat (Well of the Pigeons) was dry, and that Bir es-Sidd (Closed Well) had been ruined by falling rock. It was Thursday, 23 May, about eight in the evening; even assuming we were to have no accident, we could not be at Bir 'Ambar earlier than some time on Sunday the 26th; thus, a minimum of sixty-six hours without drink. Bah! We would meet another caravan and buy water. We met three caravans and failed to obtain a drop at any price. Friday was not too hard: I broke a piece of flint and distributed the fragments to Flaubert and our men: placed under the tongue, these activate the salivary glands and partially neutralize thirst. That night was hot and oppressive: the south wind blew, the accursed wind that Egyptian Arabs call the *khamsin* ... At four in the morning we were up, edgy and poorly rested. Laughing, I said to Flaubert: 'As Damiens said on the morning of his execution, "It will be a rough day."' We mounted our dromedaries. To protect myself against the heat, which was terrific, I wrapped my face in a thick *kufiyeh* (a coarse red cotton handkerchief striped with yellow silk); my mouth was dry, my lips mealy; vermin from my camel had invaded me and were eating me alive.* In our little caravan no one spoke—neither Flaubert nor I nor our dragoman nor our drivers, jogging along on their camels.

Suddenly, about eight in the morning, while we were passing through a gorge—a furnace—between pink granite rocks covered with inscriptions, Flaubert said to me: 'Do you remember the lemon-ice at Tortoni's?' I nodded. He went on: 'Lemon-ice is a wonderful thing. Confess that you wouldn't mind eating a lemon-ice right now.' I said 'Yes' rather gruffly. After five minutes: 'Ah, those lemon-ices! The white frost that comes on the outside of the glass!' I said: 'Shall we change the subject?' He replied: 'That would be a good idea; still, lemon-ice has much to be said for it. You fill the spoon: it's like a little mound. You crush it gently between your tongue and your palate. It melts—slowly, cooly, deliciously. It moistens the uvula; it flows over the tonsils; it goes down into the esophagus, which doesn't mind a bit, and passes into the stomach, which almost swoons with joy. Between you and me, there's a shortage of lemon-ice in the desert of Koseir!'

I knew Gustave. I knew that nothing could stop him when he was in the grip of one of his morbid obsessions, and I made no further reply, hoping that my silence would silence him. But he began again, and seeing that I didn't answer he began to shout: 'Lemon-ice! Lemon-ice!' I was at the end of my tether and had a horrible thought: 'I'll kill him!' I said to myself. I drew my dromedary up close beside him and took his arm: 'Where do you want to ride?

* He was also still in the grip of his 'indigestion,' from which, Flaubert later wrote to Louis Bouilhet, he 'almost died.'

Ahead or behind?' He answered: 'I'll go ahead.' I reined in my dromedary, and when our little troop was two hundred paces ahead of me I resumed my way. That night I left Flaubert with our men and lay down on the sand two hundred metres from the camp. At three in the morning we set out, still just as far apart and without having exchanged a word. About three o'clock the dromedaries speeded up and showed signs of excitement: water was not far off. At half-past three we were at Bir 'Ambar, drinking. Flaubert put his arms around me and said: 'Thank you for not putting a bullet through my head: in your place I couldn't have resisted.' The next morning we were enjoying something better than Tortoni's lemon-ices: we were drinking Nile water again, the equal of the most exquisite wines, especially when you have just left the desert where you punctured your waterbags.

Both Flaubert and Du Camp were given to puerile joking: in his letters to his mother Flaubert sometimes recounted their farces, *which make rather jejeune reading and have been omitted from this volume. The teasing about lemon-ice sounds not out of character. But Flaubertistes have usually called the episode improbable, pointing out that Flaubert's account of the day of Saturday, May 25, differs considerably from Du Camp's, especially in including a long if unpalatable drink at Bir es-Sidd, which was thus apparently not 'ruined,' as Du Camp says it was. In* Le Nil *Du Camp says that it was Joseph, rambling in his fever, who 'told unspeakable stories and talked rapturously about the sherbets they drink in Genoa.' There is no trace of the story in Du Camp's sixteen pages of unpublished manuscript notes on the Red Sea trip. Thus the only telling of the tale is the one printed above—by Du Camp thirty years after the event. If it happened, perhaps both men felt it too trivial to record until Du Camp, when he was sixty, and after Flaubert's death, found the story to be a 'slow burn' in his memory. Except for the complaint on page 217, Flaubert never wrote other than highly of Du Camp's companionship in Egypt.*

X

Last Weeks in Egypt

After the trip to Koseir Flaubert was stricken with a fever, which, though mild, made him particularly lethargic as far as the exploration of the remaining monuments was concerned. He made some notes on the Ptolomaic temple of Hathor at Dendera, immensely impressive and well preserved, but he did not even visit that of Sethos I at Abydos, which contains the most beautiful bas-reliefs in Egypt—though it could be said in his defense that it was at that time not fully excavated. He says in his notes, that he 'reneged' at Abydos because of fever, boredom, and a recalcitrant donkey: after starting out towards the temple he 'returned to the cange and slept all day.' After Abydos, aboard the cange, he wrote Louis Bouilhet one of his longest letters of travel-memoir and reflection—in part devoted also to criticism of Melaenis—of which selections are given here.

FLAUBERT TO LOUIS BOUILHET

Between Girga and Assiut
2 June 1850

... I have given much thought to many things since we parted, *pauvre vieux*. Sitting on the divan of my *cange*, watching the water flow by, I ruminate about my past life, sometimes quite intensely. Many forgotten things come back to me, like snatches of songs sung by one's nurse in childhood. Am I about to enter a new period? Or is it the beginning of complete decadence? And from the past I go dreaming into the future, where I see nothing, nothing. I have no plans, no idea, no project, and, what is worse, no ambition. Something—the eternal 'what's the use?'— sets its bronze barrier across every avenue that I open up in the realm of hypothesis. Traveling doesn't make one gay. I don't know whether the sight of ruins inspires great thoughts, but I should like to know the source of the profound disgust that fills me these days when I think of making myself known and talked about. I don't feel within me the *physical strength* to publish, to run to the printer, to choose paper, to correct proofs, etc. And what is that, beside the rest? Better to work for yourself alone. You do as you like and follow your own ideas, you admire yourself and please yourself: isn't that the main thing? And then the public is so stupid. Besides, who reads? And what do they read? And what do they admire?

Ah, blessed peaceful times, blessed times of powdered wigs! You lived with complete assurance, poised on your high heels, twirling your cane! But beneath us the earth is trembling. Where can we place our fulcrum, even admitting that we possess the lever? The thing we all lack is not style, nor the dexterity of finger and bow known as talent. We have a large orchestra, a rich palette, a variety of resources. We know many more tricks and dodges, probably, than were ever known before. No, what we lack is the intrinsic principle, the soul of the thing, the very idea of the subject. We take notes, we make journeys: emptiness! emptiness! We become scholars, archeologists, historians, doctors, cobblers, people of taste.

What is the good of all that? Where is the heart, the verve, the sap? Where to start out from? Where to go? We're good at sucking, we play a lot of tongue-games, we pet for hours: but—the real thing! To ejaculate, beget the child!

... Yes, when I return I shall resume—and for a good long time, I hope—my old quiet life at my round table, between my fireplace and my garden. I shall continue to live like a bear, not giving a damn about my country, about critics, or anyone at all. Those ideas revolt young Du Camp, whose head is full of quite different ones; that is, he has very active plans for his return and intends to throw himself into demoniacal activity. At the end of next winter, in eight or nine months from now, we'll talk about all this.

I am going to make you a very frank confession: I pay no more attention to my mission than to the King of Prussia. To 'discharge my duties' properly I should have had to give up my journey—it would have been absurd. I do stupid things now and then, but not of that enormity, I trust. Can't you see me in every town, informing myself about crops, about production, about consumption? 'How much oil do you shit here? How many potatoes do you stuff into yourselves?' And in every port: 'How many ships? What tonnage? How many arrivals? How many departures?' And ditto, ditto. *Merde!* Ah, no! Frankly—was it possible? And after committing a sufficient number of such turpitudes (my title itself is quite enough of one), if I had taken certain steps and if my friends had spoken for me and if the Ministry had been well disposed, I should have won the Legion of Honor! *Tableau!* Great satisfaction for my uncle Parain!!! No, no, a thousand times. I want none of it: I honor myself so much that nothing can honor me. (Pompous words!)

. . . I have seen Thebes; it's quite beautiful. We arrived one night at nine, in brilliant moonlight that flooded the columns. Dogs were barking, the great white ruins looked like ghosts, and the moon on the horizon, completely round and seeming to touch the earth, appeared to be motionless, resting there deliberately. Karnak gave us the impression of a life of giants. I spent a night at the feet of the colossus of Memnon, devoured by mosquitoes. The old scoundrel has a good face and is covered with inscriptions. Inscriptions and bird-droppings are the only two things in the ruins of Egypt that give any indication of life. The most worn stone doesn't grow a blade of grass; it falls into powder, like a mummy, and that is all . . . Often you see a tall, straight obelisk, with a long white stain down its entire length, like a drapery —wider at the top and tapering towards the base. That is from the vultures, who have been coming there to shit for centuries. It is a very handsome effect and has a curious symbolism. It is as though Nature said to the monuments of Egypt: 'You will have none of me? You will not nourish the seed of the lichen? *Eh bien, merde!*'

. . . At Esna I saw Kuchuk Hanem again; it was sad. I found her changed. She had been sick. I shot my bolt with her only once. The day was heavy and overcast; her Abyssinian servant was sprinkling water on the floor to cool the room. I stared at her for a long while, so as to be able to keep a picture of her in my mind. When I left, we told her we would return the next day, but we did not. However, I intensely relished the bitterness of it all; that's the main thing, and I felt it in my very bowels. At Kena I had a beautiful whore who liked me very much and told me in sign language that I had beautiful eyes. Her name is Hosna et-Taouilah, which means 'the beautiful tall one'; and there was another, fat and lubricious, on top of whom I enjoyed myself immensely and who smelled of rancid butter.

I saw the Red Sea at Koseir. It was a journey that took four days going and five for the return, on camel-back and in a heat that in the middle of the day rose to over 45 degrees Réaumur. That was a bit scorching: occasionally I longed for some beer, especially since our water smelled of sulphur and soap in addition to the taste of goat given it by the skins. We rose at three in the morning, and went to bed at nine at night, living on hard-boiled eggs, dry preserves, and water-melons. It was real desert life. All along the route we came upon the carcasses of camels that had died of exhaustion. There are places where you find great sheets of sand which seem to have been turned into a kind of paving, areas smooth and glazed like the threshing-floor of a barn: those are the places where camels stop to piss. With time the urine varnishes the sand and levels it like a floor. We had taken some cold meat with us, but in the middle of the second day had to abandon it. The odor of a leg of mutton we left on a stone immediately attracted a vulture, which began to fly round and round it.

We met great caravans of pilgrims going to Mecca (Koseir is the port where they take ship for Jidda, whence it is only three days to Mecca). Old Turks with their wives carried in baskets; a whole veiled harem called out to us like magpies as we passed; a dervish wearing a leopard-skin.

The camels in a caravan go sometimes one behind the other, sometimes all advancing on one broad front. When you see, foreshortened on the horizon, all those swaying heads coming toward you, it is like a horde of ostriches advancing slowly and gradually drawing together. At Koseir we saw pilgrims from the depths of Africa, poor negroes who have been on the march for a year, even two years. There are some curious sights. We also saw people from Bukhara, Tartars in pointed caps, who were preparing a meal in the shade of a shipwrecked boat made of red Indian wood. As for pearl-fishers, we saw only their canoes. Two men go in each canoe, one to row and one to dive, and they go out on to the open sea. When the diver returns to the surface he is bleeding from ears, nostrils, and eyes.

The day after my arrival I swam in the Red Sea. It was one of the most voluptuous pleasures of my life; I lolled in its waters as though I were lying on a thousand liquid breasts that were caressing my entire body.

That night Maxime, out of courtesy, and to honor his host, gave himself an attack of indigestion. We were lodged in a separate pavilion where we slept on divans and had a view of the sea; we were served by a young negro eunuch who had a very stylish way of carrying the tray of coffee-cups on his left arm. The morning we were to leave . . . I sat by myself, looking at the sea. Never will I forget that morning. I was stirred by it as though by an adventure; because of all the shells, shellfish, madrepores, corals, etc. the bottom of the sea is more brilliant than a spring meadow covered with primroses. As for the color of the surface of the water, all possible tints passed through it, iridescent and melting together, from chocolate to amethyst, from pink to lapis lazuli and the palest green, and were I a painter I'd have been very embarrassed, thinking to what extent the reproduction of those real colors (admitting that were possible) would seem false.

We left Koseir that afternoon at four, very sadly. My eyes were wet when I embraced our host and climbed back on to my camel. It is always sad to leave a place to which one knows one will never return. Such are the *mélancolies du voyage*: perhaps they are one of the most rewarding things about traveling.

As to any change that we may have undergone during our separation, I do not think, *cher vieux*, that if there is one it will be to my advantage. You will have gained by solitude and concentration; I shall have lost by diffusion and day-dreaming. I am becoming very empty and very barren. I feel it. It increases in me like a rising tide. Perhaps this is because of being physically active. I cannot do two things at once. Perhaps I have left my intelligence behind, with my draw-string trousers, my leather divan, and your company, dear sir. Where will all this lead us? What shall we have accomplished in ten years? As for myself, it seems to me that if I fail in the next thing I undertake, I might as well drown myself. Once so dauntless, now I am becoming excessively timid—and in the arts timidity is the worst possible thing and the greatest sign of weakness.

. . . Well, I hope you will agree that this letter is a veritable document and that I'm really very nice. Send me an answer to Beirut, where we'll be toward the end of July, then at Jerusalem. Work hard, try not to be too bored, don't copulate too often, conserve your strength: an ounce of sperm lost is worse than ten pounds of blood. By the way, you ask me if I consummated that business at the baths. Yes—and on a pockmarked young rascal wearing a white turban. It made me laugh, that's all. But I'll be at it again. To be done well, an experiment must be repeated.*

Farewell, old man of the pen!

... [*p.s.*] *5 June*. Tomorrow is the sixth, birthday of the great Corneille! What a session at the Rouen Academy! What speeches! ... The Academicians in full dress: white ties! Pomp, sound traditions! A brief report on agriculture!

FROM FLAUBERT'S TRAVEL NOTES

Wednesday, 12 [*June 1850*]. Arrive at 6 a.m. at el-Cheguel Guil, whence we set out to visit the Grotto of Samoun, or Crocodile Grotto.

We go by donkey to the foot of the hill, which we then climb obliquely. Splendid view of the Nile and of an immense landscape, flat, but beautiful in its very immensity, and with the low foothills in the foreground. A bit of desert—slightly rolling country. A hole, down into which we climb; we have to crawl. Sand; then very soon stones; they are large, black, slippery, sharp, hard, painful to the knees—every-

* Jean-Paul Sartre, in his detailed study of the young Flaubert, *L'Idiot de la Famille*, thinks that Flaubert did not 'consummate that business in the baths.' In his opinion, all Flaubert's pederastic talk in his letters to Louis Bouilhet is merely a form of joking, common between him and his friends; there were no homosexual relations between them as some have thought; and all the references to bardashes in the baths were the swank of a traveler wanting to impress a stay-at-home with his exotic experiences. Sartre's analysis of what he considers the evidence of all this in the letters is too long to go into here; it can be found in his first volume, pages 687 and following, and stresses particularly Flaubert's mention of the ugliness of each of the two bath attendants with whom he says he was in sexual contact (here and on p. 85), as contrasted with the others, and the fact that there is no further mention, in the letters, of the 'experiment' being repeated. Other writers differ from Sartre on this question.

thing oozes bitumen: we have to drag ourselves along flat on the ground—exhausting. If one were alone, one wouldn't go very far; fear and discouragement would win out. We twist, descend, climb: sometimes to squeeze through I have to inch ahead on my side, and several times go flat on my back, propelling myself by my vertebrae, like a snake. About two hundred paces from what might be called the mummy-stockpile, the dried corpse of an Arab that you can see clearly only as far as the trunk: the face is horribly contracted; the mouth, twisted to one side and round as an egg, is screaming with every ounce of human strength; this is an Arab who came here with a North African Moor and died no one knows how. The tradition is that they came in search of treasure and were strangled by the devil. Up until barely a few years ago, anyone who succeeded in penetrating into these caves died of suffocation after five minutes; apparently air began to blow through fairly recently. Some years ago a fire broke out and burned for a year; that is probably the reason for the kind of humidity that prevails here; bitumen oozes everywhere; it hangs in veritable stalactites from the rock; one emerges covered with tar. The Arab mentioned above mummified naturally. Our guides urge me to strain to the utmost and push myself up: I brace myself on some mummified feet, which form a threshold (the candles have gone out), and pass through.

Disorderly heaps of mummies of all kinds; the ceiling black with bitumen, the walls of the cave in deep shadow; the 'floor' is a mass of yellowish-gray mummy bandages; I sit down, panting and coughing uncontrollably.

Here they all are, one on top of another, packed together, undisturbed; their bones break under your feet; put down your hand and pick up an arm. How deep would you have to go to reach the earth ? There are as many here as the place can hold.

The way back is even harder, since we are already tired at the start. Especially the second half is over-powering—we emerge exhausted, streaming with sweat, our hearts pounding, our chests oppressed as though by burdens of several hundredweight; much of this is perhaps due to the impression of terror and weirdness. This expedition took me three-quarters of an hour and five minutes; exactly three-quarters of an hour for Maxime.

Baedeker is contemptuous of the Crocodile Grotto: '. . . hardly worth visiting, as practically nothing is to be seen except the charred remains of the mummies of crocodiles'; but Flaubert enjoyed its 'weirdness' (and perhaps the impossibility of any photography or squeez-ing being done therein). He wrote enthusiastically about it in letters to his mother and to Bouilhet, and for the rest of his life he kept in his study at Croisset a mummy's foot taken from the 'stockpile.' (He found one day that his servant had smartened it up with shoe-polish.) The reader who has been growing acquainted with Maxime Du Camp may not be surprised to find that in the Croco-dile Grotto, with its sensationalism and its call for practicality, he was, so to speak, in his element. In Le Nil *there is a lengthy account of the visit, including the following.*

FROM 'LE NIL, EGYPTE ET NUBIE'
BY MAXIME DU CAMP

And do not think, dear Théophile,* that there are

* *Le Nil* is dedicated to Théophile Gautier, and addressed to him throughout.

only human mummies there: I found mummies of snakes, crocodiles, fish, eggs, birds, animals of all kinds, all embalmed and wrapped in bandages. When you are standing on this bed of corpses, precautions cannot be too stringent: a bit of flame falling from a candle could instantly set fire to the dry debris, full of inflammable material, and then flight would be impossible and even useless. About twenty years ago an American visited the Samoun Grotto with his dragoman and a guide. Some time after he went down, a loud noise was heard, and then black smoke poured from the opening. Neither American nor dragoman nor guide was ever seen again; the fire lasted eighteen months and burnt itself out; for several years no one dared venture into the dangerous cave.

I had forbidden the guides to take the candles out of the lanterns, and I broke up some of the mummies, seeking scarabs in their bitumen-filled bellies; from one I took its gilded feet, from another its head with its long tress of hair, from a third its dry black hands. ... We returned to the *cange* by the route we had followed in the morning. My sailors and guides carried the supply of embalmed human limbs and crocodiles.

FROM FLAUBERT'S TRAVEL NOTES

Hamarna. We stop at Hamarna (not marked on the map), on Thursday, 13 June, at five in the evening: right bank.

Palms; the Nile makes an elbow; two boats are moving up-river to the right of where I am sitting. Three girls go by, all on the same donkey, the biggest near the tail, the smallest on the withers; their six legs keep knocking against the donkey to make it go. Man passing on a camel, a woman sitting cross-legged behind him. Charming landscape, broad and peaceful.

Today Flaubert would probably have more than that to say about Hamarna, now better known as Tell el-'Amarna or El-'Amarna. Excavated later in the century by Flinders Petrie, it has become famous as the remains of the city of the 'heretic' Pharaoh Akhnaton, of his beautiful wife Nefertiti, and of their artists—who worked in the unmistakable, elongated, ultra-refined style that distinguishes their painting and sculpture from all else in Egypt.

Flaubert's following entry, on Antinoöpolis, can be contrasted with Du Camp's observations about the same place when they stopped there on their way up-river (p. 108). One sees how Du Camp's description is an efficient reportage, complete in itself, whereas Flaubert looks further, interested in the question of what artistic end could be served by use of the things he sees.

FROM FLAUBERT'S TRAVEL NOTES

Friday, 14 [June 1850]. Village of Sheikh 'Abadeh (Antinoöpolis).

Arrived at eleven in the morning. Enormous, wide-branching sycamore. Nothing remains: holes, gray mounds, a palm here and there, the Arabian chain in the background. Ruins of a bath looking exactly like an Arab bath; on the ground, fragments of marble columns. In the village, on the ground, a composite capital. One column passes through the center of a house. Antinoöpolis is the ruin *par excellence*, of which one says: 'And yet, this was a city.'

Arabs come to offer us stupid curios. Little red-haired girl, wide forehead, great eyes, nose slightly flat with wide nostrils, strange face full of fantasy and animation; another little girl, dark, straight profile, magnificent black eyebrows, pinched mouth. What a charming group a painter would have made of those two children and the landscape around them! But where find the painter? And how compose the group?

Monday, 17 [June 1850]. Gebel et-Teir. At noon we are obliged to moor offshore here; it is where the Coptic monastery is situated. This time things are very mild; only two or three monks swim out to ask us for *baksheesh*. Like the first time, they're a rascally-looking lot, but our clown [Schimi] is no longer with us!

FLAUBERT TO HIS MOTHER

24 June 1850. Six leagues before Benisuef. When I wrote you my last letter, from Assiut, poor darling, I was sure that by the date I have put on this one we should already have been in Cairo several days. But I left the wind out of account. It has been constantly unfavorable to us. We have done sixty leagues in the last two weeks, and there are days when we go a mere quarter of a league even with the men working like dogs . . . Our sailors are worn thin, our *raïs* is yellow with impatience. Joseph longs to be in Cairo to send money to his wife, and Sassetti is dying to be back without knowing why—just because everybody else feels the same. In a few days our journey on the Nile will end . . .

Now back in Cairo for a week, with bad news for Du Camp, and then departure.

Tuesday, 25 [June 1850]. We sighted Cairo this morning. Our men are rowing gaily now. The Pyramids again! Gradually we meet more and more boats. In succession Roda, Gizeh, Soliman Pasha's yellow garden walls, the palace of the Grande Princesse. Bulak. We are back!

I go from Bulak to Cairo on foot . . . Cairo seemed empty and silent—an impression such as you have when you leave a stage-coach and find yourself suddenly alone in a hotel with nothing to do. I unpack the canteens and put them away. To the consulate for letters—a packet of them. Maxime's disastrous news about his lady-love!* Dinner. The table is set near the garden . . . In the evening, daguerreotypes. During the night I terribly miss the journey and the sound of the oars rhythmically striking the water. Poor *cange*! Yes—poor *cange*, where are you now? Who is walking your deck today?

Wednesday, 26 June [1850]. Pay calls. Dinner at Bulak as the guests of Raïs Farghali. Little Khalil in a silk waistcoat serves us. We dine in a low-ceilinged room, rather dark, with one corner tiled (in the back, to the left as you enter). Wonderful to have

---

* This was the coming-true of the soothsayer's prediction of bad news (p. 148). Thirty years later, in his *Souvenirs*, Du Camp still remembered the shock: 'During my second stay in Cairo, when I returned from Nubia, I had crushing news from France. I cannot express what a help Lambert was to me when he heard my confidences; I cannot express the delicacy, the marvelous art, the knowledge of the human soul with which he salved my wounds and restored my courage in the face of a misfortune of which I was the involuntary cause and which it was impossible to rectify.' What had happened was that a passionate letter he had sent to his mistress in Paris had been intercepted by her husband, who at once cast her off.

good bread again. Patriarchal character of Raïs Farghali.

All the following week: nothing! ... The conversation of Lambert Bey; aesthetic and humanitarian discussions with him on the theory of art ...

... Leaving our little boat was heart-rending. Back in the hotel here in Cairo my head was buzzing, as though after a long journey by stage-coach. The city seemed empty and silent, though in reality it was busy and full of people. The first night of my arrival here (last Tuesday) I kept hearing the soft sound of the oars in the water—that cadenced accompaniment to our long dreamy days for the past three months. The palm-trees here seemed to me so many brooms. I relived the entire trip, and in my heart I felt a bitter sweetness that was like the taste of a belch after good wine—when you say to yourself: 'Well, that was it.'

... A bizarre psychological phenomenon! Back in Cairo (and since reading your good letter), I have been feeling myself bursting with intellectual intensity. The pot suddenly began to boil! I felt a burning need to write! I was wound up tight.

... Your idea for a Chinese tale seems to me excellent in general. Can you send me the outline? Once you have decided on your main ideas for local color, do no more reading and begin to write. *Let's not get lost in archeology*—a widespread and fatal tendency, I think, of the coming generation ... Poor wretches that we are, we have, I think, considerable taste because we are profoundly historical: we admit everything, and adopt the point of view of whatever we are judging. But have we as much inner strength as we have understanding of others? Is fierce originality compatible with so much breadth of mind? Such are my doubts concerning the artistic spirit of the times, that is, concerning the few artists there are. At least, if we do nothing good we shall perhaps have paved the way for a generation that will have our fathers' boldness (I'm looking for another word) along with our own eclecticism. That would surprise me—the world is going to become bloody stupid and from now on will be a very boring place. We're lucky to be living now.

You won't believe that Max and I talk constantly about the future of society. For me it is almost certain that at some more or less distant time it will be regulated like a college. Teachers will be the law. Everyone will be in uniform. Humanity will no longer commit barbarisms as it writes its insipid theme, but— what wretched style! What lack of form, of rhythm, of spirit!

No matter. God will always be there, after all. Let us hope that He will always hold the upper hand and that the old sun will not perish. Last night I re-read Paulus's apostrophe to Venus [in *Melaenis*], and this morning I upheld (as I did at eighteen) the doctrine of Art for Art's Sake against a Utilitarian—a good man, however. I resist the torrent. Will it sweep us away? No—rather let us beat ourselves to death with a leg of our own writing table! 'Let us be strong! Let us be beautiful! Let us wipe off on the grass the dust that soils our gold buskins!'* Or not wipe them— I haven't the slightest idea what makes me quote this. So long as there is gold underneath, who cares about

* A slightly inaccurate quotation from his own *Saint Anthony*.

the dust on top? Literature! That old whore! We must try to dose her with mercury and pills and clean her out from top to bottom, she has been so ultra-screwed by filthy pricks!

FROM FLAUBERT'S TRAVEL NOTES

Monday, 1 July [1850]. Last day. . . . Farewells . . . My sadness at leaving makes me realize what elation I must have felt on arrival. Women drawing water. Fellahin I shall never see again. A child bathing in the little canal of the *'Sakyeh.*

Sultan. The people around us prevent me from being sufficiently moved by his tears of gratitude; he wants to follow us to France! I had already experienced this emotion at Assuan; perhaps that is why it was so weak here.

Bulak. Hasanin. Farewells of the sailors. The real emotion was yesterday, when we embraced Raïs Ibrahim and said goodbye.

Our last night . . . Up until three in the morning . . . Dawn. Cocks crow, my two candles are lit. I am sweating, my eyes are burning. I have early morning chills. How many nights behind me! In four hours I leave Cairo. Farewell, Egypt! Allah! as the Arabs say.

Tuesday morning, 4.05 a.m.

Friday, 19 [July 1850]. [Alexandria.] Sail for Beirut on the *Alexandra* at seven in the morning. The boat left while I was asleep: I did not see the land of Egypt disappear on the horizon. I did not bid it my last farewells . . . Shall I ever return?

Editor's Epilogue

To answer Flaubert's question: no, he was never to return. In 1858, notorious as the recently-prosecuted author of *Madame Bovary*, he was to spend a few weeks in Tunisia, around the site of ancient Carthage, for his novel *Salammbô*; and that was his only other view of the 'Orient.'

After leaving Egypt, he and Du Camp traveled through Palestine, Syria, Turkey, Greece and Italy, where Madame Flaubert met them in April, 1851, and where they separated. (They had had to renounce Persia because Flaubert had overspent.) Flaubert never forgot that it was Egypt that had given him his first 'bellyful of colors.' Writing to Louis Bouilhet from Constantinople on November 14th 1850, he said: 'Passing Abydos, I thought of Byron. That is his Orient, the Turkish Orient, the Orient of the curved sword, the Albanian costume, and the grilled window looking on the blue sea. I prefer the baked Orient of the bedouin and the desert . . . Why have I a melancholy desire to return to Egypt, to sail back up the Nile and see Kuchuk Hanem? No matter: the night I spent with her is the kind one doesn't have very often, but I enjoyed it to the full.'

That letter to Bouilhet from Constantinople is the most revelatory of Flaubert's post-Egyptian travel letters—revelatory of his literary thoughts, and, incidentally (if that word may be used), of an infection he had acquired during his travels and for which he was to have to undergo mercury treatments for the rest of his life:

'. . . We walked through (no more than that) the street of the male brothels. We saw bardashes buying sugared almonds, doubtless with money earned by their arses: the anus was about to supply the stomach with the nourishment the latter usually furnishes the former. From ground-floor rooms came the shrill sound of violins: they were dancing the *romaïque* (these young boys are ordinarily Greeks: they wear their hair very long).

'. . . I must tell you, my dear sir, that I picked up in Beirut (I discovered them at Rhodes, land of the dragon), VII [sic] chancres, which eventually combined to form two, then one. I traveled in that condition from Marmaris to Smyrna on horseback. Each night and morning I dressed my poor prick. Finally it healed. In two more days the scar will have closed. I am madly taking care of myself. I suspect a Maronite —or was it a little Turkish girl?—of having given me this present. Was it the Turk, or the Christian? Which of the two? *Problème!* Food for thought!!! This is one of the aspects of the Orient unsuspected by the *Revue des Deux Mondes!* We discovered this morning that young Sassetti has the clap (from Smyrna), and last night Maxime discovered on himself (although it is six weeks since he did any fucking) a double excoriation that looks to me very much like a two-headed chancre. If it is one, this makes his third since we began our trip. Nothing's so good for the health as travel.

'Where have you got with your muse? I expected a letter from you here, with something in verse enclosed. What has happened to China? What are you reading? What are you doing? How I long to see you!

'As for myself, I don't know just what is happening

to me as 'far as literature is concerned. At times I feel
paralyzed (the word is weak); at other times the limbic
style (style in a state of limbus and of imponderable
fluid) passes through me and circulates within me,
febrile and intoxicating. Then it ebbs. I meditate
very little, daydream occasionally. My kind of observation is preponderantly moral. I should never have
suspected this side of the trip. The psychological,
human, comic aspects are particularly plentiful. One
meets splendid types, pigeon's-breast existences very
iridescent to the eye, highly diversified as to rags and
embroideries, rich in filth, tatters, and fancy braid.
And, underneath, always the same *canaillerie*, immut-
able, unshakable. That is the foundation. Ah! How
much of it there is to be seen!

'. . . Speaking of subjects, I have three, which are
perhaps one and the same, and that worries me considerably. 1st, *Une Nuit de Don Juan*, which I thought
of in the *lazaretto* at Rhodes: 2nd, the story of Anubis
—the woman who wants to be laid by the god. That is
the loftiest, but involves atrocious difficulties; 3rd, my
Flemish novel about the girl who dies a virgin and
mystic, having lived with her father and mother in a
small provincial town, at the foot of a garden planted
with cabbages and fruit-trees, beside a stream the
size of the Robec. What troubles me is the way these
three ideas are related. In the first, insatiable love in
the two forms, earthly and mystical. In the second
the same, except that there is fucking involved, and
the earthly love is the less elevated for being more
specific. In the third, they are both combined in the
same person, and one leads to the other; only my
heroine dies of religious masturbation after practising
digital masturbation. Alas! It seems to me that when
one is as good as this at dissecting children who are

to be born, one can't stiffen up enough to create them. My metaphysical clarity terrifies me. I must get over that fear. I need, for my own sake, to know my own measure. To live in peace I want to have an opinion concerning myself, a definite opinion that will guide me in the use of my own strengths. I must know what my domain can and cannot be expected to produce, before beginning to till it. I feel, with regard to my interior literary state, what everybody of our age feels regarding his life in society: I feel the need to be settled.

'. . . To return to antiquity [in literature]: that has been done. To return to the Middle Ages: that too has been done. Remains the present day. But the ground is shaky: so where can you set the foundations? An answer to this question must be found if one is to produce anything vital and hence lasting. All this disturbs me so much that I no longer like to be spoken to about it. I am irritated by it sometimes like an ex-convict listening to a discussion of the penal system; especially with Maxime, who doesn't pull his punches and is anything but encouraging; and I'm badly in need of encouragement.

'. . . Why has the death of Balzac affected me so strongly? One is always saddened by the death of a man one admires. I had hoped to meet him later, hoped he would like me. Yes, he was a great man, undaunted by the challenge of understanding his age . . .'

Several months later he wrote from Rome, also to Louis Bouilhet: 'Back in Croisset I shall probably bog myself down in India and the great explorations of Asia. I'll block up my windows and live by artificial light. I need poetic orgies. What I have seen has made me hard to please. The *Don Juan* goes ahead slowly; from time to time a few sections are "set down in writing."'

But the *Don Juan* was never written, and the rest—the writing of *Madame Bovary*—is literary history.

Obviously, the conception of the provincial novel first thought of at Blois had deepened during the trip: it was now, in Flaubert's mind, a 'Flemish' novel—and Jean Bruneau thinks that Flaubert used the word 'Flemish' to indicate flatness: flatness of landscape, of character, of action, of tone, as opposed to melodrama or any oriental 'bellyful of colors.' It is impossible to say what role, if any, was played by what one gathers was Du Camp's constant talk to him about the modern world and 'progress'—ideas that had taken hold of Maxime since his meeting with the Saint-Simonian Lambert in Cairo. And there was the void left by the death of Balzac, the great delineator of the French provinces and modern French life; and there was all the precise chronicling he had done in his letters and notebooks.

Flaubert returned to Croisset. He re-copied his notes. (Those about Greece are inscribed: 'Finished copying these notes Saturday night, on the stroke of midnight, 19 July 1851, at Croisset.') Louis Bouilhet spoke to him about the death of Delamare. He was reconciled with his difficult mistress, Louise Colet, with some of whose traits he was to endow Emma Bovary. And on September 20th he wrote to Louise 'Last night I began my novel.'

If there are any writers among those who have read the extracts from Maxime Du Camp's books in the present volume, they will probably not be surprised to learn that after his return to France he soon became the owner and editor of a magazine, an active journalist. Relations between him and Flaubert cooled when he reproached Flaubert for his retiring way of life and urged him to come to Paris, publish something quickly, and make a name for himself. The gulf rapidly widened between one who, as Flaubert had written to Bouilhet, wanted to be settled with regard to his interior literary state, and one who wanted to be settled in society. Their relations deteriorated still further when Du Camp omitted portions of *Madame Bovary* from its installments that he published in his magazine, the *Revue de Paris*. In later years the two men became partially reconciled, and reminisced about their idyllic days on the Nile. At one of the low points of his relations with Du Camp, Flaubert wrote to Louise Colet about *Le Nil*, which Du camp had begun to serialize in his own magazine:

'Our friend Max has begun to publish his Egyptian journey. *Le Nil*, as a pendant to *Le Rhin*!* It is odd how totally insignificant it is. I don't speak of the style, which is flat beyond words, a hundred times worse than in his *Livre Posthume*.† But there is nothing in the way of meat, nothing really observed. He forgets the most characteristic natural details, those that he particularly noticed. You, who have read my notes, will be struck by this. What a quick decline!'

Louise Colet had indeed read Flaubert's travel notes, and she had read a poem that Louis Bouilhet had written about Kuchuk Hanem, based on Flaubert's letter to him about their night together, in which Bouilhet depicted Kuchuk brooding, 'sad as a widow,' after the travelers' departure. She had written Flaubert angrily, expressing jealousy of the *almeh*, and Flaubert had replied:

* By Victor Hugo.
† *Le Livre Posthume, mémoires d'un Suicidé*, a novel that Du Camp had published the year before.

'. . . Your impressions of my travel notes, dear Muse, have inspired me with some strange reflections concerning a man's heart and a woman's. Decidedly, they are not the same, no matter what people say.

'. . . As for Kuchuk Hanem, ah! Set your mind at rest, and at the same time correct your ideas about the Orient. Be convinced that she felt nothing at all: emotionally, I guarantee; and even physically, I strongly suspect. She found us very good *cawadjas* (*seigneurs*) because we left a goodly number of piastres behind, that's all. Bouilhet's piece is very fine, but it is poetry, and nothing else. The oriental woman is no more than a machine: she makes no distinction between one man and another man. Smoking, going to the baths, painting her eyelids and drinking coffee— such is the circle of occupations within which her existence is confined. As for physical pleasure, it must be very slight, since the well known button, the seat of same, is sliced off at an early age.

'. . . You tell me that Kuchuk's bedbugs degrade her in your eyes; for me they were the most enchanting touch of all. Their nauseating odor mingled with the scent of her skin, which was dripping with sandalwood oil. I want a touch of bitterness in everything— always a jeer in the midst of our triumphs, desolation even in the midst of enthusiasm.

'. . . To go back to Kuchuk. You and I are thinking of her, but she is certainly not thinking of us. We are weaving an aesthetic around her, whereas this particular very interesting tourist who was vouchsafed the honors of her couch has vanished from her memory completely, like many others. Ah! Traveling makes one modest—you see what a tiny place you occupy in the world.'

Those last words take us back to the travel notes,

especially to Flaubert's reflections on leaving Kuchuk Hanem after spending his night with her. 'How flattering it would be to one's pride,' we read in the printed notes, 'if at the moment of leaving you were sure that you left a memory behind, that she would think of you more than of the others who have been there, that you would remain in her heart!'

Did Flaubert write those bitter words that evening, one wonders, on the Nile, back aboard the *cange*, when he filled several pages of his *carnet* with his notes on Esna and the *almeh*? Or do they date from a year or so later, when he re-wrote his notes? One looks into the Nile notebook: they are not there. There, on the spot, he had contented himself with writing: 'In the morning we said goodbye very calmly.' And in his letter to Louis Bouilhet written a few days later he had said: 'Towards the end there was something sad and loving in the way we embraced.' Thus we see that the words added to the notes when he was back in Croisset are a touch of Realism, showing the way to the hard-bitten passages about Kuchuk in the letter to Louise, written when he was well launched into *Madame Bovary*.

The journey had changed Flaubert in that direction; but not all the way, and not irrevocably. Romantic echoes of Egypt are heard throughout his mature writings. In his third, final, published version of *The Temptation of Saint Anthony* (1874), the Queen of Sheba tempts the saint by saying: 'I dance like a bee'; and in his tale *Hérodias*, one of his latest works, he describes Salomé as dancing 'like the Nubian women of the Cataracts'; 'Her eyes half closed, she writhed her body above her waist and undulated her belly with a wave-like motion that shook her breasts; and her face remained impassive, and her feet never stopped.' He was so excited as he approached that scene that he wrote to his niece Caroline—the same Caroline who as a baby had been left in Madame Flaubert's care during the Egyptian journey: 'The thought of Salomé's dance inspires me with such terror that I am sick at the prospect.' One of the occasions on which poor Emma Bovary is made to seem her own worst enemy is when she lies awake foolishly dreaming, about herself and her lover Rodolphe, that 'they would live in a low flat-roofed house in the shade of a palm-tree, on a bay beside the sea'— presumably in the Orient, as the young Flaubert had dreamed in his early Romantic days. But it was the same Flaubert who, almost thirty years later, a few days before his death in 1880, wrote to his niece: 'For the past two weeks I have been gripped by the longing to see a palm-tree standing out against the blue sky, and to hear a stork clacking its beak at the top of a minaret.' 'Flaubert in Egypt' was a physical fact only for as long as his travel notes and letters have shown; as a state of mind, it continued to the end.   F. S.

Appendix

'THE CREW OF THE CANGE'
BY MAXIME DU CAMP

Raïs Ibrahim. Captain of our boat. Handsome young man of twenty-four or twenty-five, very dark, vigorous, with a short and very well kept beard rather like mine; always dressed in a blue shirt and wearing a large white turban. He had a very commanding way with his men, and drove them by simple threats: 'I'll break your arm if...' One day he struck Achmed, we never learned why; the blow cut his head open and disabled him for five days. When he went to work he was as good as ten: during the passage of the Cataracts we saw him all but split the rocks, so hard did he strike them with his pole. His usual place was in the bow, where he sometimes sat cross-legged for the entire day, looking straight ahead and occasionally calling out an order. He was very devout and regularly said his five prayers a day: not once did we know him to miss. For all his vigorous appearance, he was something of a weakling: at Minia, I think, or at Girga, we returned to the *cange* after a tour of the town to find him rolling on the deck, weeping and groaning. The entire crew was standing around him, stroking him and trying to soothe him. We hurried up, not knowing what was wrong. He had just had a tooth pulled. I gave him an opium pill. He fell into a deep sleep, and when he awoke, quite calm, I asked him how he felt. His reply was a whimpering '*Allah*

Kerim!' ('God is merciful'). On his return to Bulak he had a rather bad time. When he set out with us he had recently been married. During his absence his wife tried to kill his young brother by having him swallow a needle hidden in bread, and on his return his uncle, Raïs Farghali, made him divorce her. When he removed his turban his lock of black hair was seen to reach halfway down his back. When he was angry with the sailors he would spit at them and punch them. During the five months he was in our service he gave us not a single cause for complaint.

Mehemet Bury. (People from the Nile or the Delta are often called 'Bury'—'fish.') He was the mate: it was he who held the tiller. He was a man of about forty, one-eyed, ugly, quick with his fists, a woman-izer, very vigorous: he had once served as sailor on a merchant ship. He was an excellent swimmer. On our way down the Nile, whenever he took a hand in the rowing he electrified the crew. When rowing he liked to strip completely and utter savage cries, and the entire crew was as though inspired by him and redoubled their efforts. As soon as we landed he would always make a bee-line for the women: not that that kept him from saying all the prescribed prayers. He went in for cruel jokes. He trimmed his own beard with a knife. He used to give violent cudge-lings to Farghali,* always pretending it was in fun. In general, a disagreeable character, unwilling to accept the slightest contradiction. In the ship's concerts he played the two-reeded flute.

Hadji Ismael. Of all the sailors he was the one I

* Another member of the crew (see below). Not the *cange's* owner, who remained in Cairo.

liked best. He was very sweet-natured, with an ugly face, one-eyed, superb muscles. He posed perfectly: I always used him as a model, to establish the scale in my pictures. He jabbered a kind of gibberish that he had learned at Jidda, where he worked for a French businessman named Dubois... He was rather slack and easily discouraged. He was a Nubian.

Hasanin. A curious fellow, unpleasant, interfering, very familiar, always roaring with laughter whenever he called us Maxime or Gustave. At Assuan, while he was carrying a heavy plank, he broke his leg; we rushed to him immediately, seeing that the other men had begun to rub the leg. I set his fracture at once. He remained stretched out on the sand, and all night he kept calling us in a piteous voice: '*Cawadja! Cawadja!*' His accident had a dispiriting effect on the crew for several days. He was Raïs Ibrahim's most trusted associate.

Khalil. Former bardash. He did, in fact, have a charming behind, which we often saw when he jumped into the water with the other sailors. He played the *darabukeh* and danced. He was something of a jokester: short and slender, rather ugly, with a shifty look ... At Korosko he went off with some women while we were ashore and the boat left without waiting for him. He rejoined it opposite a spot where I had landed to shoot. He threw himself at my feet, kissed my hands, and begged me to intercede for him with Raïs Ibrahim so that he wouldn't be beaten; and I did so. I am sure that he served as wife to quite a few of the crew.

Farghali. Old philosopher. The only one who remained as fit as ever at the end of our journey, when

all the others were so exhausted as to be unrecognizable. Always cheerful, a hard worker, head oarsman
on the port side, never shirking any job except
photography, against which he had a phobia. He
couldn't bear the thought of carrying a camera, and if
asked to would put on a kind of passionate pantomime to indicate that he was good at rowing and
punting, but understood nothing about that invention of the devil. He was the hero of all the comic skits
put on by the crew. They would dress him up as a
woman, as a Pasha, and he would accept it all with
perfect good humor, even putting up with the mate's
rough jokes. One day, in a sudden rage that was quite
excusable under the circumstances, he struck the
deck-boy Aouadallah, which was something we had
expressly forbidden. Raïs Ibrahim sprang at him,
punching him and spitting in his face. Farghali sub-
mitted philosophically, saying only 'Malech'—a
verbal shrug. Another day Sassetti, leaning against the
gunwale, was drawing up water from the Nile. Raïs
Ibrahim called Farghali, who immediately lowered his
oar, striking Sassetti and knocking him down without
Farghali's noticing it. Farghali was extremely surprised that Sassetti, whom he called 'Sassetine,'
should show displeasure.

Schimi, who deserted at Assiut, at the very beginning of the trip. He was a very merry little man, an
intrepid dancer, a great mimic and teller of jokes . . .
Almost drowned every time he had to go in the water:
he couldn't swim. Showing his phallus to the Coptic
monks who swam around us at Gebel et-Teir. Lazy; a
bad sailor.

Mansur, who was taken on at Kena to replace

Schimi. Thin, rather fine, ravaged face, very debili-
tated, about forty. A fawner and flatterer, apparently
really a bad egg, very servile in his behaviour to us.
He did everything to curry favor with Raïs Ibrahim,
who seemed to dislike him—and who in general
looked down on the entire race of sailors.

Kennausi [sp ?]. Big lumpy fellow, very willing,
who worked like a horse and was stupid as a cabbage.

Hasan. A Nubian, who bore a strange resemblance
to Camille de Larinaut [a friend of Du Camp]. Very
slack, always cold, falling asleep whenever he could
and doing as little work as possible.

Mohammed, whom Gustave called Narcisse because he resembled a servant of that name he had
once had. Very hard worker, especially when the boat
was aground. The strand of hair he let grow at his
occiput was very long.

X——, whom we called Cormenin, because he
resembled Louis. Taken on, I don't remember where,
as substitute for the injured Hasanin. Strong, bony,
long-legged, gangling, always grumpy, lazy, always
backing away from any work. Forcibly kept aboard
our boat, which he wanted to leave the day after he
was hired.

Achmet. The youngest. Nubian, very ugly, face
covered with pimples. Quite a good sailor, taciturn,
something of a soothsayer, reading the future from
drawings he made in the sand. He could read and
write. On bad terms with his family because he wanted
to marry and his parents were opposed. He would

often sit in a corner for hours, saying nothing, mending his clothes.

Aouadallah. Kennausi's brother, whom we took on as deck-boy at Thebes out of charity. He had been robbed of everything he had, money and clothes, by the *raîs* he had last worked for. Quite nice-looking despite being pockmarked; was probably Bury's bardash. We outfitted him at our expense at Minia.

All our men except Raïs Ibrahim, Bury and Aouadallah had their right forefinger cut off to avoid being taken for military service.

Patras, 10 February '51.

Bibliographical Note

THE following are the principal works used in the preparation of the present volume:

Gustave Flaubert: *Carnets de Voyage*. Bibliothèque Historique de la Ville de Paris. The original manuscript notebooks kept during the journey. Never fully printed.

Gustave Flaubert: *Egypte, 1849–1850*, in *Oeuvres Complètes de Gustave Flaubert, Notes de Voyages, I*. Paris, Louis Conard, Libraire-Editeur, Paris, MDCCCCX. Also other, later editions. Printed from the manuscript of the re-written notes which Flaubert prepared in 1851 and which was sold at auction in 1931, following the death of Flaubert's niece, Mme Franklin Grout, who had inherited it. The text of the manuscript was censored, apparently by Mme Grout, before publication. It has proved impossible to trace the manuscript's present whereabouts.

The selections from the notes in the present volume have been made from both the uncensored manuscript notebooks and the printed revised notes.

Gustave Flaubert: *Les Lettres d'Egypte de Gustave Flaubert, d'après les manuscrits autographes*. Edited by Antoine Youssef Naaman, Paris, 1965.

This is the first trustworthy text of Flaubert's letters from Egypt, all previous editions having suffered from censoring, apparently by Mme Franklin Grout. I am grateful to M. Naaman and his publisher, A. G. Nizet, for permission to use this text for my selections and translations, and for much information supplied in introduction and notes.

Maxime Du Camp: *Le Nil, Egypte et Nubie*. 3rd Edition, Paris, N.D. (First edition 1852).

Maxime Du Camp: *Egypte, Nubie, Palestine et Syrie. Dessins photographiques recueillis pendant les années 1849, 1850 et 1851, accompagnés d'un texte explicatif et précedé d'une introduction par Maxime Du Camp, Chargé d'une mission archéologique par le Ministère de l'Instruction Publique*. Paris, 1852.

Maxime Du Camp: *Souvenirs Littéraires*, Paris, 1882–1883 (2 vols).

Maxime Du Camp: *Notes de Voyage. Papiers et Correspondance de Maxime Du Camp, Egypte-Grèce-Italie*. Bibliothèque de l'Institut, Paris. Du Camp's manuscript notes on the journey, on fine paper, obviously re-written in large part from whatever notes he made while traveling, and bequeathed by him to the Institut. They include also two sets of manuscript notes made during the journey: Du Camp's notes on Khalil Effendi's 'lectures,' and 'L'Equipage de Notre Cange'—'The Crew of the Cange,' as well as the signed contract for the rental of the *cange*.

In his *Souvenirs Littéraires*, Du Camp says that Flaubert finally became interested in the trip only in Greece, and that once there 'he wrote his notes every night, something he had not previously done, except here and there in Egypt. All his other notes relating to the journey were simply transcribed from mine, after our return.' That such is not the case is attested by

the existence of Flaubert's manuscript notebooks, kept during the journey. There are many
resemblances between Flaubert's notes and Du
Camp's text of *Le Nil*: it was apparently the
habit of the two friends to write some of their
notes together, as on the rug in Memphis
(p. 58). But Flaubert was quite right in telling
Louise Colet (p. 219) that his notes were very
different in character from Du Camp's printed
account; and the same difference exists between
them and Du Camp's notes that are still in manuscript. Furthermore, contrary to what Du Camp
says, Flaubert's Greek notes in the notebooks are
less voluminous than the Egyptian. The sparsest
of his Egyptian notes in the notebooks are those
on Thebes; but his fuller, printed Thebes text
could not have been 'transcribed' from Du
Camp's Theban notes—at least as the latter exist
today; they bear no resemblance to them.

Jean Bruneau: *Les Débuts Littéraires de Gustave
Flaubert, 1831–1845*. Paris, Armand Colin, 1962.

Jean Bruneau: *Gustave Flaubert: Les Sept Fils du
Derviche, Conte Oriental*. Text and commentary.
Paris, Éditions Denoël, 1972.

I am much indebted to those works and also
to Professor Bruneau's generous response to
requests for additional information and opinion.
It was he who kindly supplied me with the full
text of Flaubert's letter to Louis Bouilhet of 14
November 1850, which when the present volume
was being prepared had not yet been printed in
the Pléiade edition of the *Correspondance de
Gustave Flaubert, I*, edited and annotated by
Jean Bruneau (Paris, 1972). (The Pléiade super-
sedes all other editions of the letters, which, with

the chief exception of M. Naaman's edition of the letters from Egypt, are greatly marred by the censoring that was apparently done by Mme Franklin Grout.)

My thanks go also to Madame Olivier Ziegel, Norbert Guterman, the Bibliothèque Historique de la Ville de Paris, and the Bibliothèque de l'Institut.

Readers who may know my *Flaubert and Madame Bovary* and *Selected Letters of Gustave Flaubert* will find certain differences—improvements, I hope—in the translation of certain passages in the present volume. Spelling of Arabic and Turkish words has been taken from Lane, Naaman and Baedeker.